Official Know-It-All Guide™

CAREER PLANNING

Anna Mae Walsh Burke, Ph.D., J.D.

Frederick Fell Publishers, Inc.
2131 Hollywood Blvd., Suite 305, Hollywood, FL 33020
Phone: (954) 925-5242   Fax: (954) 925-5244
Web Site: www.Fellpub.com

Fell's Official Know-It-All Guide

Frederick Fell Publishers, Inc.

2131 Hollywood Boulevard, Suite 305

Hollywood, Florida 33020

954-925-5242

e-mail: fellpub@aol.com

Visit our Web site at www.fellpub.com

Library of Congress Cataloging in Publication Data

Burke, Anna Mae Walsh.
 Career planning / Anna Mae Walsh Burke.
  p. cm. -- (Official know-it-all guide)
 ISBN 0-88391-062-4 (Paperback : alk. paper)
1. Vocational guidance. 2. Career development. I. Fell's official know-it-all guide. II. Title.
HF5381 .B7763 2002
331.7'02--dc21

2002007911

10 9 8 7 6 5 4 3 2 1

Graphic Design: Elena Solis

Dedication

To those who are my life and love,
Who put up with my long hours on the computer
And requests for proofreading at inconvenient times
My husband Bob, my son, Rob, my daughter, Ann, and Grandma whose
memory supports me in everything I do.

Table of Contents

Introduction

At the time I wrote my first book on careers, I was an administrator at a University in charge of a number of undergraduate and graduate programs. I became concerned about many of the students in these programs who were returning to school after a long absence. In spite of the fact that they were making great personal and financial sacrifices, many of these students had not clearly thought out their career goals. My concern resulted in my writing three books, *Returning: A Survival Manual for Women Returning to School, What Do You Want To Be Now That You're All Grown Up, and How to Choose A Career Now That You're All Grown Up.*

During many of the personal appearances I made in connection with these books, I discussed career decisions with young people who were just starting out as well as with returning students. Many of the young adults had just finished expensive educational programs, but they had either not chosen a career or were not happy with their choice of career. In many cases they were trapped by having to repay large educational loans and did not have the freedom to make another choice. In addition, having once made the "wrong" choice, they were very fearful of choosing again. Students who were just beginning college appeared to be just as confused by the career choices they had before them. They all needed help but were uncertain as to where it could be found.

The present book discusses the choice of a career whether it be a first career or a new career and the means of preparing for it. In addition to the careers that have been around for centuries, new careers appear to be created every few seconds. How do you find out about these new careers? How do you train for them? How can the Internet help you find careers? And, most importantly, how do you decide which career is the right one for you? This book will discuss all of these issues with you as the focal point.

You have taken the correct first step by selecting this book but it won't do you any good if you simply let it sit on the shelf. If you want to be successful in selecting a career that is right for you, do the exercises in each chapter beginning with chapter one. Good Luck!

Chapter 1
Choosing a Career

When my cousin learned that she and her husband had won an Irish lottery, the first thing she did was call him on her cellular phone. He was driving a truck between Dublin and Belfast as he had done for his own company for many years. "When will you be home?" she asked. "When I finish delivering my load," he said, surprised that she thought he would do anything else. He likes his work and the money they won has not changed their lives to any great degree. Before getting all of those Irish pounds, they had a lovely home and a good business. They have mostly invested the money for their future and that of their daughters. Many people who win lotteries or inherit large amounts of money behave in the same way. It is not only professionals who continue with the job they had been holding for many years rather than relying on new found wealth to obtain happiness. Of course, some who had always hated their jobs will stop working. They have been dreaming of a chance to free themselves from a job they disliked for years.

Whether you are just starting out in a career or whether you are changing careers, the question remains the same. How do you know if the career you select will make you happy? Will it continue to satisfy you as the years pass? Will you be disappointed that you didn't choose something else to do with your life? How do you find a career that you would continue to work at even if you won the lottery? While there are no certain answers to these questions, are steps you may take to insure your success in picking a career.

The selection of a career is one of the most important choices you will make in your life. It is second only to the selection of a spouse. You may work at the career you select the rest of your life, day in and day out. That sounds dreadful doesn't it? It is if you make the wrong choice. Your daily activities as well as your potential income will depend on your making the right choice now.

Years ago, many young women graduating from high school or college looked for something that would be transitional, just a job to work at until they got married. This is not the case any more. It is not only the man or the "career woman" who must select a career for a lifetime. Today, most women work for much of their lives and the more they like their work, the happier their lives will be just as it is for the men they marry.

Whether you are a young adult just starting out to select your first career or a more mature individual, you must be thorough in your selection. Yes, I did say "first" career, for many if not most people will have several careers in their lifetime. Please remember that changing careers is not a sign of failure. It may demonstrate maturity or a newly advanced level of education. It may be related to the new opportunities and types of work that are constantly opening up. The new career may be one that did not even exist at the time the person chose their first career. Changing is not failure. The development of technology, for example, is continuously expanding the number and types of careers available.

The prospect of making a commitment to a career can be frightening. Family, friends, and even school guidance counselors are not necessarily the best people to assist you in making this choice. The best person is yourself.

When you were a child did anyone ever pinch your cheek and ask you "What do you want to be when you grow up?" You might have answered that you wanted to be a fireman or ballet dancer or a teacher or an astronaut. Whatever you said, it was based on what you thought somebody did in these careers and how exciting that job would be for you. You didn't know much about these careers unless somebody in your family had one of them. You didn't know exactly what these people did every day. You didn't know the scary aspects of being a policeman or fireman. You didn't understand the hours of practice needed to be a ballerina. You also didn't know what kind of a livelihood one of these careers would bring you. Pensions were probably something you had never heard of. You certainly didn't know the kind of education or training you had to have to become whatever it was you said you wanted to be.

Now that you are selecting your first career, you may find yourself as ill-equipped to answer that question as you were when it was posed to you all those years ago.

You may have held part-time or summer jobs while in high school or in college or even held a number of full-time jobs. From these you should have learned some of the personal aspects of working. You may have had to learn about getting along with co-workers or working for a boss who does not understand or appreciate you. You may be brighter than the person who gives you orders. Even if you choose the "right" career, these factors may always be present in any job you may hold in the future.

The basic principles of selecting a first career or changing a career are the same except that people changing a career must think about what that change will mean in their lives and the lives of their family. The person selecting their first career must think about the kind of lifestyle that will be provided by that career. This lifestyle will be dictated not only by the income produced by the career but the time constraints it will impose. Will you always have to work the hours of the lawyer in *The Firm* ? Will the job require considerable travel such as would be necessitated by a job as an airline steward or stewardess? What kind of a family life would you have if you choose that career? Would your life be glamourous? Would it be exciting? These are just some of the elements you must consider in choosing a career.

Your career will be a basic building block of your life. Whether you are selecting your first career or changing your career, it is important to consider if the life dictated by that career is the one you actually want. If you are changing careers, what will happen to your old life? Changing to a new career may require that you introduce many changes into your lifestyle. This will be discussed in the next chapter. This

11

book will help you to evaluate your present and future career potential and to understand how to maximize your skills and interests in selecting that new career. It will also teach you how to undertake the steps necessary to get the first job in that new career area. But it can only accomplish these things for you if you fully participate in the activities.

This book does not assume anything about you and you should not assume things about yourself. You may have held some jobs in the past, no matter how basic they were and you must examine what you learned about yourself from these jobs if you are looking to change your career or choose your first career. Don't neglect delivering papers, babysitting, or working in a fast food restaurant when thinking about the jobs you have held in the past. These were not big money makers, but the money you earned was certainly important to you at the time. It may have been the only reason you took these jobs. You will be asked to analyze these jobs to determine what you really like to do.

12

You took the first step in finding the right career for yourself when you opened the pages of this book. It was written for you, not for anyone else. This is not simply a general book intended to fit everyone but which may fit no one. It is a book that specializes in finding the right career for YOU.

The Focus is on You

In order for this book to really be about you, you must free yourself of any resistance you may feel. You must put yourself into the book. This book will not ask you to do anything foolish or embarrassing. It will, however, pose a lot of questions for you to answer. Your responses will involve some deep questioning on your part about many topics, some of which are very personal. Some of these topics may be very sensitive to you. Others may seem to be irrelevant. Whichever the circumstances, answer the questions you are asked with care. These answers will be used in decisions you will make in exercises in later chapters. They will be important in the decisions you ultimately must make regarding career choice. All of these questions fit into the larger purpose of helping you shape your future by your choice of career. This book will not give you all of the answers, because only you can fill in those blanks. It will, however, help you to find the right choices for you.

Making Your Career Selection a Positive Experience

In order to make your selection of a career a positive experience, you must approach it with an open mind and consider all possibilities. Technology is the source of many new work opportunities that you may never have considered. The typewriter, a self-contained mechanical device, is a recent invention in the history of mankind. As long as it was in the making, however, the simple manual typewriter was quickly replaced by the electric model. When I wrote my first books in the early 1980's, it was still unusual for a writer to have a personal computer, but I did. I wrote in those books about sitting in my living room and writing my book on my own computer. In a book I did on computers for young people called *Microcomputers Can be Kidstuff*, I included photographs of my own children using computers because such pictures were not readily available from the manufacturers. In fact, the publisher of my second book used my computer disk, a big eight-inch floppy, to experiment with typesetting the book. It is now standard practice in the area of publishing for the writer to submit the book manuscript on disk to the editor. Not all books are produced on paper any longer. Some books are now in an e-format available on computer disk or able to be downloaded to a computer or a hand held reader. This is known as e-publishing. The last book I published, I wrote on a laptop computer which works on a rechargeable battery as well as with A.C. I used it to write on the beach, the patio, in the car, on the top of a mountain, and even on a ferry between Ireland and England. For this book, I am using software whereby I can dictate to the computer and the computer understands my words and they come flying back at me across my computer screen. It is very accurate and the more I use it, the better it understands my speech. The word processing program I am using is much faster

13

and has many more options than I could even dream of in 1980. It even underlines my spelling mistakes in red as I type. That can be intimidating.

For other book projects, I have used a portable scanner which was not much larger than a stapler and which cost less than my printer, to scan in material I had previously written and photographs and drawings I have made. With my flatbed scanner, I scan in photographs as well as text and drawings and download from my digital camera. I can draw on the computer and color my drawings on the screen. No crayons anymore! Some of the material I have written in the past still exists on paper and on the big, old eight-inch or five and-one-quarter-inch floppies which won't run on any of the computers I currently own and so I use my scanner to update this material for use on the computers I now use. Those early computers and their floppies are already dinosaurs although they are only twenty years old. I have used my modem to connect to various data bases so that I can down-load information I need. The Internet seems to have taken over our lives and will be discussed in a separate chapter. People of all ages are sending e-mail, including digital photographs, all over the world and getting back information on topics that are interesting to them. This is a dramatic change in the twenty or so years I have had books published. It is symptomatic of the extraordinary changes that are taking place because of advances in technology and changes in both business practices and social institutions. While the invention of the personal computer was certainly a positive change for me, it may have had a negative effect on those who found that they had to learn to use a computer in order to keep their jobs. Today, auto mechanics use computers to diagnose problems as well as to calculate bills. Grocery clerks take the store inventory as they ring up sales. Seamstresses use elaborate (and expensive) computerized sewing machines to produce clothing. The patterns for needlepoint can be worked out on the computer and then printed for use. Many medical tests involve the use of computers. At present, it is almost impossible to think of a career that doesn't involve some use of computers. We cannot predict with any accuracy what will be the next stage. The list is endless and so, therefore, is the list of your possible careers.

Tipping the Odds in Your Favor

You can tip the odds of selecting the right career in your favor by making choices after careful planning. You can't just stick a pin in a list to perform your selection. This is true whether you are just entering college or in the middle of your life. Mid-life career change is not a new phenomenon. It is an age-old problem. A few people associate this experience with such intense degrees of fear, regret, depression, and/or anxiety that mental illness has been the result. Psychologists have long used "mid-life crisis" as a descriptive term for this phenomenon. In our world of "pop" psychology, this term has been applied to any one who is considering a change in career, a new lifestyle, etc. People even apply it to themselves. An apparently well-balanced gentleman, with whom I had lunch recently, used the term to fill me in on what he had been doing during the past two years. "I've been having my mid-life crisis," he said. "I changed my wife and my job and went back to school." That isn't a misprint, he really did say "wife", not life. I have no way of knowing the degree of trauma he really suffered, but I still have a feeling he meant "change" rather than "crisis." Change can be good or change can be bad. Mid-life change is no different from an early life crisis. Indeed, it may be a mixture of both —a bittersweet process. Everyone wants to believe that his or her problem is unique. Most people don't want to consider certain aspects of their lives a problem. They do not understand that many suffer the same misgivings they do. They do not understand the process of making a transition. The secret of a successful change lies in the way in which the transition is made. Many are insecure about the process of making a change. They believe they are alone. They do not understand that many others have gone through the same process and they do not understand that change can be a good thing. They unconsciously cry out, "Don't give me a label or a lecture. Tell me what to do." This book is intended to teach you how to find your own solutions, not just follow a recipe.

Exercise 1.1

Write down five things that you would like to achieve in your life in the coming year.

1._____

2._____

3._____

4._____

5._____

Exercise 1.2

Write down five things that you would like to achieve in your lifetime.

1._____

2._____

3._____

4._____

5._____

Exercise 1.3

Write down five things that you expect to achieve as a result of reading this book.

1._____

2._____

3._____

4._____

5._____

Exercise 1.4

Are any of these things the same?

1._____

2._____

3._____

4._____

5._____

Chapter 2
The Role of Change
in Your Life

W hile the element of change is greater for a person undergoing a mid-life career change, the effect of change on a person selecting a first career cannot be ignored. You may have set yourself in a certain career direction and have chosen a college and academic program based on that initial choice. Your parents may be assisting you financially based on that initial career choice. They may want you to be a doctor or a lawyer rather than an artist or an actor. But you may now determine after the analysis described in this book that your first choice is not the career you now desire. It is therefore important to understand the role of change in your life.

Have you ever thought of the sound of the word "change"? It has a brittle sound-the sound of a battle axe hitting a piece of armor, the sound of a bell breaking the stillness of the night, of a wire snapping, of a glass breaking. A brittle sound. The sound of change washes across our lives bringing joy and sadness. It is long, drawn out single-syllable word, "change". Some people see change as inevitable. Others see it as desirable, while still others see it as disastrous. We cannot avoid change but we can shape what it does to our lives.

Sometimes we choose the change. Other times it is the result of outside forces.

Sometimes change chooses us. The rate of change around us has increased dramatically in our lifetime. There are individuals who watched men land on the moon in July of 1969 who were alive when Orville and Wilbur Wright made the first flight. While much of the world watched that first moon flight, few now are even aware of the launching of space shuttles unless some disaster occurs. There are those who watched the first moon flight who may be so bored by present shuttle flights that they begrudge a little television time from a sports event to report a launch. The rate of change is so great that it causes boredom to set in too quickly. If we don't move from crisis to crisis, our attention span wanes.

Remember that change can be both positive and negative. What place does the word "change" have in your life? Are you being forced into change by circumstances? Are you ready for change? Are you craving it? Are you afraid of it? How can you take advantage of it? There is no doubt you will continue to be affected by changes, and there are many things you can do to prepare for them.

18

As a society, we have begun to pay more attention to changing roles for women. Today the question of change is an equally important one for both men and women. Times are changing for everyone. Many young men are becoming more involved in the raising of their children. At the same time, many young women have managed to find the path that will ultimately cause the glass ceilings to shatter in the business world. Women no longer believe the limits that society has long imposed on their career choices. Both men and women are stretching themselves to grasp new opportunities both in their personal lives and in their career choices.

There have been many changes since I wrote my first two books, *Are You Ready? A Survival Manual for Women Returning to School* and *What Do You Want To Be Now That You're All Grown Up*, but only a few of those changes are due to legislation. Social pressure has brought about many of the changes. Often changes are due to a growing realization on the part of both men and women that they can reach their potential if they try. For many people, going back to school is a large part of the answer, but it is only a part. If you do not respond to change, you will get run over, perhaps without even realizing it. Much of this change is the result of technological advances. Once brute strength is eliminated from a task, there is no reason some woman cannot do it as well as some man. Indeed, it must be recognized that some women are stronger than some men, so even the issue of brute strength is false. Law schools and medical schools have women enrollment figures that are much higher than would have been projected thirty years ago. Women have surged ahead in many technical areas. Women are no longer accepting limits that were imposed on them years ago and men are realizing that they should do the same.

The Reasons for Career Change

Whatever your feelings about the women's movement, its effect on both men and women cannot be ignored. It has caused people to focus on various aspects of their lives and relationships. Many men as well as women are beginning to take a serious second look at their lives and lifestyles. A major question these men and women have to answer is one of career change. For some, this career change results in a dramatic lifestyle change. For others, the change is neither dramatic nor traumatic. Superimposed on many positive aspects of modern careers has been the tremendous down-sizing of corporations. This euphemism for "layoffs" has been a disaster for many, especially workers in their late forties and fifties. Finding a new job continues to be a difficult task for workers in this age group. The answer for them has often been to find a new career; but finding that new career, training for the new career, and finding a job in the new career has still been difficult for many, coupled as it often is with depression, insecurity, and disbelief. Downsizing has also caused difficulties for young people who are just leaving school as well as for people changing careers. The career they had planned may have been de-railed while they were in school or perhaps they had never really considered any particular career and now they just can't find a job, not to mention select a career.

Do not feel that you are alone in thinking about selecting a career. Desire to change a career or do something unusual are not new, but it was only under special circumstances that people were able to change careers in days gone by. A serf, (male of course), who was tired of tilling the soil of England and wanted a more adventurous career might have found himself going on a Crusade but he didn't have much to say about the matter. Whether he stayed on the farm or went off to war, the choice was really out of his hands, being made for him by the lord of the manor. Men could not easily rise "above their station" even in much later times. There was no choice at all for women. Remember, Maid Marion had to take to Sherwood Forest to escape her fate, and she still ended up as a housewife even though her husband was Robin Hood and she didn't even have a house.

For you, the words, "rising above your station" must be recognized as meaningless. Today, a person is limited only by his or her talents, imagination and drive. You may argue this is not so, but you know it is true. People do get out of the ghetto. Some poor boys do grow up to be millionaires. These days both men and women get to be doctors and judges as well as movie stars and sports figures. Discrimination, poverty, prejudice, and good old boy attitudes do keep some people down, but not everyone. While not everyone succeeds, many do. How do they do it? That is what you must learn. The person who succeeds can be you and must be you. But to do it, you must plan and you must be motivated and confident.

No one who is selecting a career can afford to make mistakes, but this is especially true for the older person. The young person who is just starting out has much less to lose. It has been predicted that today's graduates will make at least three career changes in their lifetime. The more mature adults may already have a life and a lifestyle which must be protected during the process of career change. They also have obligations which must be met while all of this change is taking place. Even those selecting a first career may have lifestyles that need to be maintained. Many college students are already married with families who must be considered in the decision process.

Freedom to Choose Change

There is always the fear that the new career and the new life may not be as good as the old one. Do you remember the two figures in the painting *American Gothic*?

20

A man and a woman, images of each other, standing side-by-side, a pitch fork held staunchly in front of them, a farm scene behind them. They seem to be the personification of a steady, unchanging life, yet they existed at a time when there was considerable change on the American frontier. People moved from the stability of cities and towns in the East to gain a chance at a new life in the West. The pioneers were by no means all young. Many were heads of families. For some, the journey was a success and they found a new life. Others met failure and sometimes even death.

You have the freedom to choose. You may be the solid figure of American Gothic, content, unchanging, bored, or you may change and either succeed or fail. Fate cannot take all the credit for your failures. Studies have shown that the most successful people take credit for their failures. Please notice that I didn't say successes. I said failures. These people don't spend their time pointing fingers at others or stating reasons why they couldn't succeed. They admit their failures and go on. Begin to keep some notes about things you have learned from this book. Write down this sentence, "I will admit my failures to myself, and spend no more time thinking about them." An important element of your change is to move on.

For those who are changing jobs, there may be a number of reasons which have caused you to make this change, some of which you may not even be aware of. There may be different specific career opportunities in which you have become interested. This book will help you sort out those opportunities and make some choices.

While the purpose of this book is to help you explore your life and your interests, identify possible "right" careers and goals, and plan for a positive change in your life, it will also help you assimilate the results of changes which you cannot control. You may have been seriously considering a change in your life. That change may be dictated by circumstances such as graduation from high school or college. Or it may be dictated by a divorce. It may only be a nagging restlessness, a secret wish, or it may have taken a stronger form. You may already know what aspects of your life you would like to change.

One of the major changes you may be considering is a different career. This kind of change has a tremendous impact not only on many aspects of your own life, but

21

also on the lives of those around you. It will impact on family relationships. It will change your lifestyle and your finances. It may cause you to move or to go back to school. It may, and probably will, cause changes in every facet of your life. If this is a first career, it may mean you are "getting out of the nest." You may have finished college without picking a specific job. There are many subjects you can major in which have no relationship to the career you ultimately choose. There are many jobs you could obtain which would not require a certain major in college or even much specific training. You may major in art history or the classics and go into sales or become a stockbroker. There is a certain amount of training necessary for these jobs, but the education required is not a four year college degree with a specific major. Certain careers such as real estate broker or stockbroker require licensing and training for the examination but do not require a college degree. If you are considering a new career, it is important that you plan very carefully. This book has been written to help you make this change a positive experience. Remember that change can be both positive and negative.

22

What place does the word "change" have in your life? Are you being forced into change by circumstances? Are you ready for change? Are you craving it? Are you afraid of it? How can you take advantage of it? There is no doubt you will continue to be affected by changes, and there are many things you can do to prepare for them.

As a society, we have begun to pay more attention to changing roles for women. Today the question of change is an equally important one for both men and women. Times are changing for everyone. Many young men are becoming more involved in the raising of their children. At the same time, many young women have managed to find the path that will ultimately cause the glass ceilings to shatter in the business world. Women no longer believe the limits that society has long imposed on their career choices. Both men and women are stretching themselves to grasp new opportunities.

There have been many changes since I wrote my first two books, *Are You Ready? A Survival Manual for Women Returning to School and What Do You Want To Be Now That You're All Grown Up*, but only a few of those changes are due to legislation. Societal pressure has brought about many of the changes. Often changes are due to a growing realization on the part of both men and women that they can reach their potential if they try. For many people, going back to school is a large part of the answer, but it is only a part. If you do not respond to change, you will get run over, perhaps without even realizing it. Much of this change is the result of technological advances. Once brute strength is eliminated from a task, there is no reason some woman cannot do it as well as some man. Law schools and medical schools have women enrollment figures that are much higher than would have been projected two generations ago. Women have surged ahead in many technical areas. Women are no longer accepting limits that were imposed on them years ago and men are realizing that they should do the same.

Stop and think about the way you want change to enter your life.

Exercise 2.1

If you could change five things in your life, what would you choose?

1._____

2._____

3._____

4._____

5._____

Exercise 2.2

Why do you want to make these changes?

1._____

2._____

3._____

4._____

5._____

Exercise 2.3

Can you make some of these changes now?

1._____
2._____
3._____
4._____
5._____

Exercise 2.4

Would changing careers or finding a first career help you to make these changes?

1._____
2._____
3._____
4._____
5._____

Chapter 3

Stress as a
Way of Life

When did you last pick up a magazine that didn't have an article on stress? "Exercising to Control Stress", "Eating to Control Stress", "Don't let Stress Destroy Your Marriage", "Take Vitamins (tranquilizers, listen to the sound of the surf,) to Reduce Stress", etc. etc. etc. You can't avoid the topic, but thinking about stress is itself stressful. Stress is seen to be a dominant component of American life. It has, in fact, become a way of life. Women used to live a significant number of years longer than men but that gap is slowly closing due to added stress in women's lives. To some degree stress is a valuable component. There are those who believe that a certain amount of stress is a necessary and valuable part of the successful life. It keeps you stimulated. It keeps you going! Nevertheless, it is important that you learn to control stress. If it gets out of control, it can adversely affect your health and your relationships with family, friends, and co-workers.

You will want to study how you react to stress and competition. In choosing a career, you may want to select a career that has a minimum amount of stress or competition. You may thrive on stress. You may desire high levels of competition. Athletes are good examples of the latter type of person. They may say that they are competing against themselves, doing their best, but in fact they are competing against their opponent as well and this gives them the surge necessary to do their best.

In any case, you should minimize the stress that attaining a career adds to your life. You cannot avoid the fact that you will be uncertain that you are choosing the best career for you, but continual planning should bring you some confidence as to the validity of your choice.

An important aspect of controlling stress is to minimize unnecessary tension in your life. In a classic study done a number of years ago, psychologists attempted to develop a scale, called the Holmes-Rahe Scale, to rate stress according to a point system. One could simply total up the points for the things that applied to his or her lives. Too many points indicated that the subject could be in trouble. An important thing to remember is that good and positive things cause stress as well as negative things. If we take a look at some of the point ratings on the Holmes —Rahe Scale we will understand better how a career change will dramatically add up the points so that your life may reach a crisis stage. The most traumatic experience identified by the scale, the death of a spouse, is rated at 100 points. (See Table 1). Divorce is close behind. A major change in arguments with a spouse is a 35. Financial changes are also high. A wife starting or ending work is a 26, major changes in family get —togethers is a 15. Failure is a 43; outstanding personal achievement is a 36. The beginning or end of formal schooling is a 27. Illness is a 44. A number of the scores are work related. Being fired is a 47. Retirement is a 45. Business adjustment is a 39. Change to a different line of work is a 36. Major change in work responsibilities is a 29. Trouble with the boss is a 23. A major change in working conditions is a 20.

Certain things are a tipoff as to how old the test is. Who has a mortgage less than $10,000.00? Many students graduating from college have loans totaling forty or fifty thousand dollars. This was unheard of in the 1960's. Some students graduating from law school today have loans in the ninety thousand dollar range. They have the price of a home on their backs before they even graduate. Medical students have even greater loans to pay back for their education.

While the scale could use an update in terms of certain numbers, the items are still well chosen. The last item listed above, "Minor violations of the law" registers when you are stopped for a speeding violation. Few would deny that seeing that red and blue light flashing behind you is certainly an example of stress.

26

I have selected only some of the stress-triggering situations that may develop as a result of a career change or finding a career. You can even collect a number of points by only "thinking" about changing careers.The Holmes-Rahe Scale uses 300 points collected over a period of a couple of years as a critical number to measure stress in your life.

Little Things Mean a Lot

Recent studies on stress have shown that the repetition of certain relatively minor situations such as housework, whining children, boring chores, constant nagging either at home or at work, or remarks made by work associates and supervisors, repeated daily and cumulatively, may even be more stressful than the items listed in the table above. Think of all the points you could be adding up. There may be family difficulties. You may have financial changes. The stock market is up or down. You think of stocks you should have bought as well as stocks you shouldn't have bought. You may both begin and end school. You may have difficulties with your husband or wife, in-laws, parents, children, boss, co-workers, or a friend. You may have to cut down on family get-to-gethers if your time is taken up with training for the new career while keeping your old job. You may get all the work-related points. You may get points for both failure and success or beginning or ending school or work.

You must have the idea by now. Selecting or changing a career is a very stressful activity. You must minimize your stress components if you are to maximize your chance for success. How to do that will be discussed in a later chapter.

Change is a process of gain and loss. Part of the process of selecting a new career is a thorough estimate of what you will gain and what you will lose. Do the gains outweigh the losses, not just in number but also in quality? Can you live without the things you will be surrendering? Can you live with the things you will be gaining? Change implies transition. You do not wake up one morning with everything instantly changed. Pieces of your life will change at different rates: something old, something new, something borrowed, something blue. Some people cannot face the transitions. Some people cannot survive them. Planning the change means planning transition.

27

Getting the Most from this Book

If you are going to get the best results from this book, you will have to work on all the exercises. These will help you to obtain the information about yourself that you will need to make the best possible career change.

Put together a notebook of your answers. You may want to keep this notebook private or you may want to share it with those whom you trust and who have confidence in you.

Exercise 3.1

Write down the items from Table 1. The Social Readjustment Scale that have occurred in your life during the past year. If you run out of lines, just add a few.

Incident   Points

_____

_____

_____

_____

_____

_____

_____

Total Points _____

How did you make out in terms of points? Are you heading for the magic 300 even though we only considered this past year? Along with choosing a new career we will work at reducing the stress in your life so as to optimize the process of changing to that new career.

Exercise 3.2

Write down 10 things (or more) in your daily life that are causing you daily stress.

1._____

2._____

3._____

4._____

5._____

6._____

7._____

8._____

9._____

10. _____

How many points would you associate with each stress factor in your life? Write the numbers you choose on the list above. Both of these exercises will be used later in the book but keep the numbers in mind as you go through the rest of the exercises. While you may be raising the stress level of your life, it should be on a temporary basis.

Are you ready to begin looking for that new career? How do you know if you are ready? If you are to be ready for change you must understand many things about yourself, your present life, and your relationships. Perhaps most importantly, you will have to make a very careful choice of a new career.

Exercise 3.3

What ten things can you do to minimize the stress in your life which you listed in the two questions above?

1._____

2._____

3._____

4._____

5._____

6._____

7._____

8._____

9._____

10._____

Table 1 Social Readjustment Rating Scale

Rank	Life Event	Mean Value	Rank	Life Event	Mean Value
1	Death of a Spouse	100	23	Son or daughter leaving home	29
2	Divorce	73			
3	Marital separation	65	24	Trouble with in-laws	29
4	Jail term	63	25	Outstanding personal achievement	28
5	Death of a close family member	63			
			26	Wife begins or stops work	26
6	Personal injury or illness	53	27	Begin or end school	25
7	Marriage	50	28	Change in living conditions	24
8	Fired at work	47	29	Revision of personal habits	24
9	Marital reconciliation	45	30	Trouble with boss	23
10	Retirement	45	31	Change in work hours	20
11	Change in health of family member	44	32	Change in residence or conditions	20
12	Pregnancy	40	33	Change in schools	20
13	Sex difficulties	39	34	Change in recreation	19
14	Gain of new family member	39	35	Change in church activities	19
			36	Change in social activities	18
15	Business readjustment	39	37	Mortgage or loan less than $10,000	17
16	Change in financial state	38			
17	Death of a close friend	37	38	Change in sleeping habits	16
18	Change to different line of work	36	39	Change in number of family get-togethers	15
19	Change in number of arguments with spouse	35	40	Change in eating habits	15
			41	Vacation	13
20	Mortgage over $10,000	31	42	Christmas	12
21	Foreclosure of mortgage or loan	30	43	Minor violations of the law	11
22	Change in responsibilities at work	29			

Source: Holmes, T.H., and Rahe, R.H. The Social readjustment rating scale. Journal of Psychosomatic Research, 1967, 11, 213?218.

30

Chapter 4
Who Are You?

*I*n kindergarten, thoughtful teachers give a child a box of crayons and ask him or her to draw a picture of themselves and of their families and homes so that they can learn about the child's concept of self. Child psychologists do the same thing to identify disturbed or abused children. In this chapter, I won't give you any crayons but I will ask you to take your pencil and write the answers to the questions scattered throughout the chapter. We are not looking for any psychological problems but simply trying to perform a huge task, helping you to understand you.

How many times when you were a child did people ask you, "What are you going to be when you grow up?" Someone may have pinched your cheek while asking the question and your answer may have been mixed with a wish that you were somewhere else. Now you are asking yourself that same question. Can you remember your answer? If someone were to ask you that same question now, what would you say? Are you planning your life or are you just letting it happen?

Remember the childhood game —rich man, poor man, beggar-man, thief, doctor, lawyer, Indian chief." Looking back, the words now sound more like the members of a rock group than real choices. In the past, the career choices for men as well as for women were often as limited as the words in that game.

Many of the choices were jobs, not careers. They were, for the most part, the same jobs that the people around you held. It is not necessarily a matter of following in your father's (or mother's) footsteps, although that certainly does take place. What sociologists call "role models" shaped our choices over the years as they still do today. It is a matter of knowing about different jobs and of having different job opportunities. At one time in your life, you may only have known about certain jobs because you knew people who had those jobs. Children often want to be teachers or firemen because they know what teachers and firemen do. They seldom want to be environmental specialists or mechanical engineers unless they know about those jobs from people around them. When you were growing up, there probably was little opportunity for you to find out about the different kinds of careers that were available. How could you make a choice when you didn't know what the choices were? You may not even be aware of the career opportunities that exist today.

Job vs. Career

Words are interesting, powerful tools for understanding more about ourselves. The difference between the word "job" and the word "career" is an ocean of pride, income, and often independence. Let us explore Webster's Intermediate Dictionary for the meanings of the word job and the word career.

32

Webster defines a job as a duty, or a task, or a position at which one regularly works for pay. It defines career as a profession pursued as a permanent calling. A *career* is alternately defined as a course of continued progress or activity. The first two definitions are what you might expect. It is the third one that is really important to us in our investigation. When I use the word career, I mean it in a much broader sense than just the designation of a few professions such as law, teaching, nursing, and medicine. On a day-to-day basis, a career is a job, but continued movement and development is inherent in it. In some cases, a career denotes progress within a field after some entry level position. In other cases, for example, in medicine, law, nursing, and science, you may have to have certain educational credentials and possibly pass a state sponsored licensing examination. A career generally has many stages which may differ in degree of responsibility, creativity, complexity, financial reward, or some characteristic intrinsic to the position.

When I use the word career in the remainder of the book, it is in this broader sense. When you select a new career, think of all the stages. Look at them, for example, at five-year intervals. What will you be doing five, ten, fifteen, and twenty years from now, if you choose a particular career? Does that career have a single track or are there many places in which the career can branch? What kinds of decisions must be made at the branch points? Do all of them lead to things which you like to do? How much of a choice do you have with regard to these branch options?

Because we cannot accurately predict the future, this analysis may seem to be a futile task, but some effort must be made to project the future stages of the career you select. How stable are those career areas in the technologically volatile world in which we live?

Some individuals who are reading this book have been forced to change careers because the jobs they held were phased out. This may be happening in the company they work for or it may be happening in the industry as a whole. If that job was a link in a career chain, the career itself may have taken a completely different turn or have been eliminated. The most recent material which I have read indicates that college graduates can expect to have two or three totally different careers in a lifetime. Some people do not think of themselves in terms of a career, but it is important that they begin to do so. Just "holding a job" becomes increasingly difficult in today's world. Inflation is rarely met by cost of living raises and merit raises are almost non-existent. The principal process for financial movement seems to be movement on the career ladder. In technical areas it is often related to moving from one company to another. If you have "fallen off the ladder" because of economic or technological changes and you want to stay in that same general work area you may need retraining in order to jump the gap and catch up with your career. If the career area you have chosen has disappeared, you may have to change careers entirely. If you have not yet gotten on a career ladder, you may be asking yourself if that is the ladder you want to spend the rest of your life climbing.

Finding Your Professional Goals

These concerns cause us to focus on a new term, that of "goals." What are your professional goals? Your goals are your objectives, the conditions in your professional life which you would like to achieve. A good salary, having a number of people report to you, freedom to design your own projects, and an ability to work independently are all examples of professional goals. These goals may be translated into specific positions on the career ladder you have chosen. You may want to be a company president or vice president, or a head designer, or a lawyer with a private practice. You will have to establish some professional goals within your career field as well as select a specific career.

Men are often asked, "What do you do for a living?" Women are still more likely to be asked if they are married, if they have children, or possibly, where they work. The association of the word "career" with the word "woman" is not readily made by either men or women. Whether you are a man or a woman, you must associate the word "career" with yourself rather than your just having a job.

34

Don't ever think it is too late! What did we know, you and I, about choosing a career when we were growing up? Nobody even called it a career when I was growing up. It was, "what would I be?" Your total person is more than just your career selection but your total being is a much larger topic than we shall try to answer here. The selection of a new career may indeed be part of the creation of a new self and a new self-image. The question of career is often not addressed soon enough in a person's life. Choosing courses or a major in college which do not lead to a career can often be an expensive mistake. Are you making that mistake now?

In some respects, self and self-image cannot be separated as demonstrated by the rather broad range of questions asked below. The use of the answers however will be limited to the selection of a new career. Although you may have many ideas occur as a result of the questions presented later in this chapter, the essential question on which we will focus and which you must answer for yourself is, "Now that I am all grown up what do I want to be? What career do I want to choose?"

Identifying Positive Aspects of Your Most Recent Job

Why did you start thinking about choosing a career? Are you dissatisfied with your current job? Is it just a job or does it have some elements of a career as defined above? Do you believe that what you do every day is what you really want to do for the rest of your life? If someone asks you what you do, how do you feel when you answer? Is there pride, excitement, and enthusiasm or do you answer in a few mono-syllables and quickly change the question? Have you reached a point in your education, such as impending graduation from college, when you must make a decision? Shouldn't you have made that decision before now?

Try this test question. If you were a guest on a television program and had to tell the whole country what you do for a living, how would you feel? How would you describe your job? What would you call it? Would you be proud, ashamed, embarrassed or just neutral? Are you able to describe your job or the job you intend to pursue to other people? What words do you use to tell others what you do or plan to do? What tasks would you do all day in this job? Do you really know what they are? Are they creative or monotonous? Do you have to deal with certain types of people or activities that you dislike? Are there some parts of your job that you like? Are there some parts that are exciting to you?

The Key Questions

Let us move to a key part of the question: "Now that you're all grown up. . ." Take a look at all those words. After you have completed the process of thinking about these aspects of your life, we will move on to filling out some questionnaires. I have found that some people are hesitant to write things down unless they know where the questions are leading. They like to peek at the back of the book to see how it will come out. As this is your life, there is no place to "peek" for the answer, but the process of thinking first and then writing the thoughts down helps many people to gain confidence in the process.

WHAT

Exercise 4.1

Do you know already just what new career you would like to have?

_____

Exercise 4.2

If you could choose any career, what would you select?

_____

Exercise 4.3

What was the first thing that came to your mind in answering question 4.2? Is that what you wrote down or did you write down another answer after some additional thought? What was your instantaneous answer? It may be important to include this answer in later discussions.

_____

Exercise 4.4

Are there old dreams to be reckoned with? What are they?

_____

Exercise 4.5

How will you know which career is the right one for you?

_____

_____

Exercise 4.6

How can you find out?

_____

_____

Exercise 4.7

Are there careers you never thought of as being suitable for you? What are they?

_____

_____

Exercise 4.8

Did the right career for you even exist when you were starting out? This is a valid question whether you are in midlife or just starting out. New careers seem to be springing up every day.

In the case of many, especially women, are you only really starting out now?

Have you been just holding jobs and now want to move to a real concept of a career?

DO

Remember that "DO,"is an action word. Now is time to take action. Your first step is reading this book.

Exercise 4.9

List ten things that you are able to do with self-satisfaction. It might be write, paint, throw a football, raise children, add a column of figures, etc.

1. _____
2. _____
3. _____
4. _____
5. _____
6. _____
7. _____
8. _____
9. _____
10. _____

Exercise 4.10

Do you like doing them? Which ones do you like best?

_____

Exercise 4.11

Which ones do you dislike doing even though you may be good at them?

_____

Exercise 4.12

What do you think are your real abilities?

_____

Exercise 4.13

Do others in your life know and value these abilities?_____

_____

38

Exercise 4.14

What kind of changes in your abilities can you carry out?

_____

Exercise 4.15

What kind of training or formal education will develop your abilities so that you could perform adequately in the new career?

_____

Exercise 4.16

What kind of changes in your life are you really willing to carry out in order to reach goals you will set for yourself?

_____

_____

_____

YOU

Exercise 4.17

Who are you?

_____

Exercise 4.18

Have you ever really thought about yourself?

_____

Exercise 4.19

How do you describe yourself?

_____

Exercise 4.20

How do others describe you? (Include your family, your friends, your teachers, your current work associates?)

_____

Exercise 4.21

How do you believe you would appear to prospective new employers?

_____

_____

_____

_____

Exercise 4.22

Are there things that you would like to change about yourself?

_____

Exercise 4.23

Are these things external changes or internal changes? Which is which in your view? _____

Exercise 4.24

What kind of changes would you like to make in your appearance?

_____

Exercise 4.25

What kind of changes would you like to make in your speech?

_____

Exercise 4.26

What kind of changes would you like to make in your attitude?

_____

Exercise 4.27

What kind of changes would you like to make in your credentials?

_____

Exercise 4.28

How do you go about changing yourself in all of these ways?

_____

_____

_____

WANT TO BE
Exercise 4.29
What kind of things do you like to do?

_____

Exercise 4.30
What kind of new careers would you like to explore?

_____

NOW THAT YOU'RE ALL GROWN UP
Exercise 4.31
What does it mean to be an adult?

_____

_____

41

Exercise 4.32
If you are still in school, do you consider yourself an adult?

_____

Exercise 4.33
Do others look on you as an adult in terms of the way you take responsibility for your actions?

_____

_____

Exercise 4.34
Are things different about changing careers because you are an adult?

_____

Exercise 4.35

What kinds of responsibilities cannot be changed in your life?

_____

Exercise 4.36

What would a career change mean in your life?

_____

Exercise 4.37

What would a career change mean to those people who are in your life?

_____

_____

_____

42

Dreaming of Escape

For many, Paul Gauguin represents the ultimate in mid-life career change. He went from being an ordinary man with a wife and child and a job in an office to being an artist on the island of Tahiti, living a free and unbounded life. For some people, this would seem to be the ideal life. They do not necessarily want to paint under the breadfruit trees, but may be seeking to escape responsibility and lives that have become very mundane. Others may be afraid to even consider a change because they feel it implies a desire to run away. These people are not seeking to avoid responsibility but secretly want to find a career, and ultimately a life that is more satisfying. They may be afraid family or friends will think they are trying to escape responsibility. They may even be secretly afraid that they are trying to escape responsibility. Some who are just selecting the first career, may be looking to reduce their degree of responsibility or they may be afraid to select an "exciting" career for fear that others will laugh at them. In some families it is not acceptable to be an actor or an artist. Others do not see the value of education. I had a friend once who wanted to be an actress but her father wouldn't permit it so she became a teacher, respectably acting every day.

People who dream of Tahiti may need a certain amount of courage, but they do not need to make the kind of plans we will be discussing. Those who are concerned about finding balance in their lives will find they need to plan any change very carefully. We are not planning for escape. We are planning for success.

What Does It Mean to Be an Adult?

The question of being "grown up" is one that deserves some exploration. What does it mean to be an adult? What is the first thing that pops into your mind? If you ask a teenager, you might get an answer that focuses on driving a car. If you asked a person burdened by family responsibilities, the answer might focus on that aspect of life. Duty has been taken on by many to a great degree. This duty may involve a husband and children, elderly parents, or substantial debt. Very often these duties appear to stop individuals from making changes that are good for them. What they forget, most often, is that if the changes are good for them, they will most likely be good for the people around them.

All aspects of adulthood don't happen simultaneously. The first aspect is the biological definition of adulthood —that time when you have the ability to reproduce. This definition comes into effect years earlier than any of the other definitions. While it is a definition, it is not sufficient for most people.

The second is a legal definition. The laws for marriage, voting, the draft, driving, drinking, making contracts, etc. designate various ages for the legal definition of adulthood. These may vary from state to state and from country to country, yet all take the position of relating legal adulthood to a specific age. A friend, who is also an attorney, told me of the problem she kept having with a client who would not sign a Marital Settlement Agreement which obliged him to pay support until his child reached majority. He demanded that she change the word majority to maturity. He was wrong, of course, the correct word was majority. State law defines majority at a

43

specific age. In most states it is eighteen. Maturity is a stage that some people never seem to reach and it would be very difficult to determine if a person had indeed reached maturity. There is no test for it. This definition of adulthood is not completely satisfactory either.

The third definition of being adult links adulthood to the sociological aspects of man. When do you start performing adult roles, such as worker, citizen, family head, father or mother? This definition is extremely important in a career change. The process of change may result in your moving to what might be considered a "non-adult" role for a period of time, for example, that of student or apprentice. You have certain sociological aspects to your life. You may be a respected member of your community because of what you do. Will this be maintained in the career change? Will your sociological aspect be enhanced? Initially? Ultimately? What new role will you take in your sociological family?

The fourth definition of adulthood is a psychological one. Do you think of yourself as an adult? This question may be especially important for women who entered a home role at an early age and have not functioned as an adult in certain psychological or sociological ways. Whether you are conscious of it or not, as an adult you have established a set of values for yourself and your life. These values may have a moral component or they may be related to religious feelings and feelings concerning morality. They may have an economic component, relating to money and the things money can buy. They may have a personal component which is related to the manner in which you interact with people and even the fact that some people are important to you. What is important to you? Who is important to you? What is most important? Yourself, other people, things you create, money, power, God. Everyone has a list and the list changes according to the circumstances. What would you do to obtain various objects, people, possessions, or positions? This is where your personal set of values comes into place. You will have to think about your set of values. They will be important when setting your professional goals. How will you decide what will be important in the selection of a new career?

44

How Do You See Yourself?

What is your perception of yourself? Are you happy with yourself as an adult? Self-analysis is very difficult, even when it is limited to the question of career choice. How do you look when you stand back and hold yourself out at arms length? Will you avoid some answers to certain questions because you are afraid of them? Have you been avoiding certain topics with regard to yourself for years? Have you created some buffers so that you do not have to admit certain things even to yourself? It will be important to begin with analyzing yourself. If this does not seem to be working, you may have to turn to professional help.

For some individuals, a career change or the selection of a career different from the one you have been considering is a way of changing their total life. The real reason you want a new career is something you will discover for yourself as we move through the process of identifying a new career and the way to achieve it.

If you have a habit, as I do, of checking magazine counters to see what is being published, you may find articles with checklists and little self-surveys that will tell you what is wrong with your life, or what is right with your life, or what color you should dye your hair, or how to take inches off your waistline, etc. Some of these articles and questionnaires are quite useful, not only because of the information contained there, but also because they make you consider certain questions in relation to your own life.

I don't believe in giving point values to things and adding up your life like a bingo game, but I do believe it is possible to draw out some things you may not have been aware of, through the use of lists. The creation of different lists will be an important part of the process of identifying a new career and taking the necessary steps to achieve your goals.

Take your notebook, a pad of paper, and a pencil to a quiet, comfortable place where you will not be interrupted or under any time constraints. I said a pencil rather than a pen so you can erase and change your mind to your heart's content. You may not be able to finish this exercise in one sitting. It is probably better if you

45

come back to it several times and refine your lists over and over. Remember that you are planning your future, and possibly that of your family. Do not think of this as a silly exercise. It may be very important to you.

I am not assuming I have thought of all possible questions. If you can think of questions that are more meaningful for you, please use them. This is your exercise. This is also your life.

Although this book is primarily about selecting a first career, remember that a change in career may have a profound effect on other aspects of your life and the lives of those around you. Before identifying a new career area, let us examine the basis of your desire for change.

46

Chapter 5
Study Yourself First!

PUTTING YOURSELF UNDER THE MICROSCOPE

Before you begin to study the career areas, you must first study yourself. Perhaps you may feel that I am putting you under a microscope just to make you wiggle a little, but all the wiggling that you will do, will be done for yourself alone. These exercises are important and for that reason, they have been grouped into a chapter by themselves. Begin this chapter when you have some time for yourself and some privacy. These exercises require that you be honest. Don't show them to anyone unless you are very comfortable with that person. Try and set aside enough time to complete a good portion this chapter at one sitting because the exercises are related. If you do have to stop, read over what you have written before you begin again. If you want to make some changes on previous questions, go right ahead. There are no right answers here, no passing grades. It is only a series of exercises that should get you to know yourself better, and to better understand how to change your live in a positive way by the choice of a new career.

Exercise 5.1

What are the things that you like best about your life?

Write down as many things as you can think of. Include at least ten answers. Don't write down what you think the magazines or your minister or your mother would want to hear. What are the things that you really like best about your life? Write the best of the best as number 1, the next best as 2, and so on.

1._____

2._____

3._____

4._____

5._____

6._____

7._____

8._____

9._____

10._____

48

When I was a little girl, like lots of other little girls of my generation, I read a book titled *Pollyanna*. Disney has made this book into a movie. Pollyanna was a beautiful little girl who was quite poor and who had been taught by her missionary father to look for the good in every happening. It was symbolized by the fact that when a pair of crutches came in the missionary barrel instead of the doll she wanted so badly, she expressed her thankfulness that she did not need the crutches. Our times have become so cynical that it is an insult to call someone a "Pollyanna" yet it is important to find the positive elements of one's life and job.

While an attitude of sunshine and light is not very functional in present times, the cynical attitude which replaces it is not always very useful either. The good things in a person's life may have been adversely affected by change simply because they were not considered in the change process. You cannot change some things in your life without affecting everything else to some degree. Many people who have carried out substantial changes have found that while they did eliminate or improve some things they did not like, they also adversely affected some things they did like. Don't neglect listing the good things in your life that are important to you and which you do not want changed.

Exercise 5.2

What are the things you like least about your life?

You may want to write these down very privately. Even those who love you may react strangely if they see some of the things you write down. Be honest with yourself -- considering a career change may really be part of a larger picture. Write down at least 10 things, worst is number 1 in this exercise.

1._____
2._____
3._____
4._____
5._____
6._____
7._____
8._____
9._____
10._____

Exercise 5.3

What things in your life would you change if you could?

Although you may think that this question is the same as the previous item, your answers may not be identical. There may be changes that you would like to make that didn't make the list of things that you like least about your life. It is also possible that you may not want to change certain things you like least about your life. These things may involve people whom you love. You may not want to change some of the things that you don't like about yourself. Although the latter may seem strange, psychologists will tell you that this is often the case. Put the thing that you would most like to change as number 1 and so on.

1._____
2._____
3._____
4._____
5._____
6._____
7._____
8._____
9._____
10._____

Exercise 5.4

Which of the things listed in the two previous questions are you most likely to be able to change?

Do not forget to list things that could really be changed even if they mean training or education, or some change in your surroundings or lifestyle. I would like to be taller but that is one characteristic which is not likely to be actually changed. I am not going to grow taller, no matter how hard I wish for it. List ten things, with most likely as number 1.

1._____
2._____
3._____
4._____
5._____
6._____
7._____
8._____
9._____
10._____

The People in Your Life

Exercise 5.5

Who are the people in your life at the present time whom you love the best?
Don't forget to hide your list. You can have ties among your rankings here and that may make you feel better about ranking the ones you love. You don't have to fill in all of the blanks in this questionnaire but you can go over the ten lines if you wish. Peek ahead at the next question where you are asked to list the people you like. Distinguish between like and love in this question, but you can repeat the same people for the next few lists.

1._____
2._____
3._____
4._____
5._____
6._____
7._____
8._____
9._____
10._____

Exercise 5.6

Who are the most important people in your life at the present time?
These may not necessarily be the people you love the most. In fact, there may be people on this list who make your life miserable. A terrible boss, a jealous co-worker, a person for whom you have a great burden of responsibility or guilt, but little love.

1._____
2._____
3._____

4._____
5._____
6._____
7._____
8._____
9._____
10._____

Exercise 5.7

Who are the people in your life now whom you like best?

This is another list you should hide from others so that no one is offended and so that you can be honest with yourself. You are allowed to have some tied places. It is hard to decide among people.

1._____
2._____
3._____
4._____
5._____
6._____
7._____
8._____
9._____
10._____

Exercise 5.8

Who were the people you have liked in former years?

For many of us, life was different when we were young. We may have lived in a very different part of the country and have done different things. The people we knew then may be quite different and perhaps have different values than the people who surround us now. Is your desire for a change related to this? Life may have been easier then. Who were the people you liked in years gone by? How do the values these people demonstrated relate to your own values and professional goals?

1._____
2._____
3._____
4._____
5._____
6._____
7._____
8._____
9._____
10._____

Exercise 5.9

What characteristics do the people in exercises 5.7 and 5.8 have that makes you like them?

The question of the difference between the terms "like" and "love" is often raised. There are those whom we love whom we may not like very much and there are those whom we like and admire whom we do not love. If you are fortunate, you like and love some of the same people and they like and love you back. Think of the characteristics of those you like and those you love. Write them in on the list below. Think of the reasons you like or love them. Is it because of these characteristics? You may have more or less than ten answers in this exercise.

1._____
2._____
3._____
4._____
5._____
6._____
7._____

8._____

9._____

10._____

Exercise 5.10

Are there some of these characteristics which you wish you possessed?

The characteristics which you have written down above may be the reasons you like these people but they may not be characteristics which you desire to have yourself. Write down ten of the characteristics which these people have which you want to try and develop with the one you want most to develop as number 1. You can have more or less than ten answers.

1._____

2._____

3._____

4._____

5._____

6._____

7._____

8._____

9._____

10._____

Exercise 5.11

How do you think the most important people in your life see you?

If the most important people in your life, whom you identified in Exercise 2.7, were to make a list of your most important characteristics what would they write down?

1._____

2._____

3._____

4._____

54

5._____
6._____
7._____
8._____
9._____
10._____

What About You?

Exercise 5.12

What characteristics do you like best about yourself?

This is an important question. Remember that this is not the time for false modesty. If you think that you are very intelligent, beautiful or friendly and this is important to you, admit it, at least to yourself. List at least ten things.

55

1._____
2._____
3._____
4._____
5._____
6._____
7._____
8._____
9._____
10._____

Exercise 5.13

What characteristics do you like least about yourself?

This is equally important. Once more, list at least ten things. Remember, don't show your lists to anyone. You want to study your own feelings and attitudes and you must be clear about them. Many people will feel this the most difficult assignment. We try to hide our weaknesses even from ourselves. It is a matter of our own survival. Some of the things you don't like about yourself may be causing you problems in your old work area and can obstruct you in your new career choice.

1._____
2._____
3._____
4._____
5._____
6._____
7._____
8._____
9._____
10._____

Exercise 5.14

Are there additional characteristics you wish to possess?

These characteristics may be physical, emotional, psychological, or educational. If ten spaces are not enough, make a longer list, but write down at least ten characteristics.

1._____
2._____
3._____
4._____
5._____
6._____
7._____
8._____

9._____

10._____

Exercise 5.15

What could you do to develop these characteristics?

Write something for each characteristic you have written above. You can write just a few words or whole paragraphs. You may return to this exercise over and over. It is not an exercise which you can complete in a few minutes or which can be done without really giving serious thought to come up with some workable answers.

1._____

2._____

3._____

4._____

5._____

6._____

7._____

8._____

9._____

10._____

The Effect of Career Change

Exercise 5.16

How would it affect those whom you love or like or who are the most important people in your life if you developed those characteristics?

Write down a few words or a paragraph for each characteristic. You may be very surprised at the results. Some people whom you love may like you the way you are and may be resentful or jealous of changes that you may make. Others may feel that they will lose your love if you make these changes. Would the changes be good for them? If you do select a new career what will it mean to these people? If you are considering different careers, what will the impact of each of these careers be on these individuals? Take as much space as you need to write these answers.

1.＿＿＿＿＿＿＿＿＿＿＿＿＿＿＿＿＿＿＿＿＿＿＿＿＿＿＿＿＿＿＿＿
2.＿＿＿＿＿＿＿＿＿＿＿＿＿＿＿＿＿＿＿＿＿＿＿＿＿＿＿＿＿＿＿＿
3.＿＿＿＿＿＿＿＿＿＿＿＿＿＿＿＿＿＿＿＿＿＿＿＿＿＿＿＿＿＿＿＿
4.＿＿＿＿＿＿＿＿＿＿＿＿＿＿＿＿＿＿＿＿＿＿＿＿＿＿＿＿＿＿＿＿
5.＿＿＿＿＿＿＿＿＿＿＿＿＿＿＿＿＿＿＿＿＿＿＿＿＿＿＿＿＿＿＿＿
6.＿＿＿＿＿＿＿＿＿＿＿＿＿＿＿＿＿＿＿＿＿＿＿＿＿＿＿＿＿＿＿＿
7.＿＿＿＿＿＿＿＿＿＿＿＿＿＿＿＿＿＿＿＿＿＿＿＿＿＿＿＿＿＿＿＿
8.＿＿＿＿＿＿＿＿＿＿＿＿＿＿＿＿＿＿＿＿＿＿＿＿＿＿＿＿＿＿＿＿
9.＿＿＿＿＿＿＿＿＿＿＿＿＿＿＿＿＿＿＿＿＿＿＿＿＿＿＿＿＿＿＿＿
10.＿＿＿＿＿＿＿＿＿＿＿＿＿＿＿＿＿＿＿＿＿＿＿＿＿＿＿＿＿＿＿

Exercise 5.17

How would these changes affect your choice of a new career? Would these characteristics be important in the new career? This question may seem to be more related to changing your total life than an assessment of a new career, but many times they are closely related.

1.＿＿＿＿＿＿＿＿＿＿＿＿＿＿＿＿＿＿＿＿＿＿＿＿＿＿＿＿＿＿＿＿
2.＿＿＿＿＿＿＿＿＿＿＿＿＿＿＿＿＿＿＿＿＿＿＿＿＿＿＿＿＿＿＿＿
3.＿＿＿＿＿＿＿＿＿＿＿＿＿＿＿＿＿＿＿＿＿＿＿＿＿＿＿＿＿＿＿＿
4.＿＿＿＿＿＿＿＿＿＿＿＿＿＿＿＿＿＿＿＿＿＿＿＿＿＿＿＿＿＿＿＿
5.＿＿＿＿＿＿＿＿＿＿＿＿＿＿＿＿＿＿＿＿＿＿＿＿＿＿＿＿＿＿＿＿
6.＿＿＿＿＿＿＿＿＿＿＿＿＿＿＿＿＿＿＿＿＿＿＿＿＿＿＿＿＿＿＿＿
7.＿＿＿＿＿＿＿＿＿＿＿＿＿＿＿＿＿＿＿＿＿＿＿＿＿＿＿＿＿＿＿＿
8.＿＿＿＿＿＿＿＿＿＿＿＿＿＿＿＿＿＿＿＿＿＿＿＿＿＿＿＿＿＿＿＿
9.＿＿＿＿＿＿＿＿＿＿＿＿＿＿＿＿＿＿＿＿＿＿＿＿＿＿＿＿＿＿＿＿
10.＿＿＿＿＿＿＿＿＿＿＿＿＿＿＿＿＿＿＿＿＿＿＿＿＿＿＿＿＿＿＿

Analyzing Past Jobs

Exercise 5.18

What kinds of jobs have you held in the past?

Include everything from your first job (paid or unpaid) to your present one. Don't forget to include volunteer or elected positions.

1._____
2._____
3._____
4._____
5._____
6._____
7._____
8._____
9._____
10._____

Exercise 5.19

What did you like best about each of these jobs?

Once more include at least ten things about the jobs. Are some of these things the same for several jobs? Has some of your dissatisfaction with different jobs been repeated a number of times?

1._____
2._____
3._____
4._____
5._____
6._____
7._____

8._____
9._____
10._____

Exercise 5.20

What were the things you liked least about each of these jobs?

Again, make your list as complete as you can.

1._____
2._____
3._____
4._____
5._____
6._____
7._____
8._____
9._____
10._____

Exercise 5.21

What were the things that you could do best in these jobs?

1._____
2._____
3._____
4._____
5._____
6._____
7._____
8._____
9._____
10._____

Exercise 5.22

Have you ever been fired, laid off or almost fired from a position?

Have you ever admitted to yourself exactly what happened when you were terminated? Did the situation repeat itself? Why? You cannot always have had a boss "who was out to get you" or peers who were jealous. What elements are you putting into the situation? Are you repeating your failures without learning from them? Think about this very carefully. If you have a recurring problem in this area, you may need some counseling to clarify the situation.

1._____
2._____
3._____
4._____
5._____
6._____
7._____
8._____
9._____
10._____

Exercise 5.23

Rank your jobs in order from the best to the worst.

Did some of the jobs which were at the top of the list have some of the same "best characteristics?" What were some of the common characteristics of the worst jobs?

1._____
2._____
3._____
4._____
5._____
6._____
7._____

8._____

9._____

10._____

Exercise 5.24

What were the best characteristics of the jobs you have had in the past?

Use all of the lists from Exercises 5.18 through 5.23 to put together this list. You may have had more independence in one job and a good salary in another. Your list may be very different from someone else's even though they may have held similar jobs in the past. One person's dream job is another person's nightmare. The important thing is to isolate some of the characteristics of a job, and ultimately a career, which are important to you. The next two items will help you rename some of the elements which either should be present or absent in a new career.

1._____

2._____

3._____

4._____

5._____

6._____

7._____

8._____

9._____

10._____

Exercise 5.25

What are ten characteristics you would like to have associated with your new career? This is a very important list and will be used to a large extent in the next chapter. Write down whatever number is comfortable for you. It is important however to generate enough characteristics to make the exercise useful. You can use the information which you have generated in Exercises 5.18 through 5.24 as well as all of the characteristics that you can think of but which you have not had in other jobs. Perhaps a higher salary is one, or more responsibility, more freedom, being your own boss, working outdoors, working indoors, working with people, working by yourself, doing creative things. These are only a few basic things. People's lists will be very different.

1._____
2._____
3._____
4._____
5._____
6._____
7._____
8._____
9._____
10._____

63

Dreaming Your Dreams

Exercise 5.26

What are your number one dreams?

This is an emotional getaway list. If you could do or be anything in the world, what would you choose? Put it on your list. Have you had any dreams in the past?

Put them down. Remember, there are no constraints-- no lack of time or talent, youth, agility, or burden of other responsibilities. You are not too old or too clumsy nor do you have too many other responsibilities. You can be an astronaut, a ballet dancer, a doctor, a teacher, a judge, a movie star, a hero or heroine, a great artist, a writer, a bulldozer operator, a high-wire walker, or a sea captain.

Anything goes on this list.

1._____
2._____
3._____
4._____
5._____
6._____
7._____
8._____
9._____
10._____

Exercise 5.27

Which of the "number one dreams" do you have some possibility of fulfilling?

The next step is to survey this list of dreams and remove to a second list those for which you have absolutely no talent or historic indication of attaining. Do not remove any dreams just because you lack training or education. If you are changing careers, it is most probable that you will have to undergo some formal training in order to be prepared. Notice that I did not say eliminate them. I did not say cross them out or laugh at them. I said remove them. Call the list of remaining dreams "number two dreams."

1._____
2._____
3._____
4._____
5._____
6._____
7._____
8._____
9._____
10._____

Exercise 5.28

What would you really like to do if you could?

Is there anything left on your list of number one dreams? If so, you are lucky. Many people face a blank piece of paper at this point. You may think that what you have left on your list is exactly what you want to do but you owe it to yourself to research your new career a little more. Write down what you have left on your list. I have given you ten lines, but you may have far fewer things to list there. Don't worry. The point of the exercise is to cut down on your choices.

1._____
2._____
3._____
4._____
5._____
6._____
7._____
8._____
9._____
10._____

65

Exercise 5.29

The next step is to supplement your lists. Begin with some of the topics you put on the second list. Are there some things on the list that, although impossible in themselves, might suggest some realistic goals to you?

For example, you may never be an astronaut, but is there some way you could work in the aerospace industry? Could you be a scientist or could you be a computer programmer for the National Aeronautics and Space Administration (NASA)? Could you begin as a secretary in an aerospace company that does aerospace work and develop some expertise? Could you move up in that company to a position of responsibility? Could you report on space and other science activities as a technical journalist or could you be an artist who works for a publisher who does science fiction or hard science books? This form of networking can go on and on. The result will be different for each person but the process will be the same.

1._____
2._____
3._____
4._____
5._____
6._____
7._____
8._____
9._____
10._____

Your interests may be very different. You may never be a ballet dancer, for example, but is there some role you could have with a ballet company or with a civic cultural center which you might enjoy and to which you might bring some expertise and enthusiasm. You may teach appreciation courses or fund raise for cultural projects. These may be extreme ideas, but I think you understand what I mean. Add these related career possibilities to your list.

Exercise 5.30

Now begin to add those activities that appeal to you and for which you may have more ability to achieve than the ones you eliminated from your original list. After you have written down all the things you can think of, you should turn to other sources for ideas.

1._____
2._____
3._____
4._____

5._____

6._____

7._____

8._____

9._____

10._____

Chapter 6
Where Do You Look for New Careers?

*I*n searching for the right career, you have to keep your mind open to interesting areas which you may never have considered before. Some careers you will immediately discard as being wrong for you. I do not wish to be a big game hunter and I don't have the physical characteristics necessary to be an astronaut. For me these are obvious discards, but don't discard careers because you don't know what the person does or because you would need some training. Find out what a person specifically does in these careers and what training is needed.

Your next task will be to make lists of careers that interest you, some of which may be traditional ones while others may relate to opportunities that didn't exist even a few months or years ago.

While it is important to learn about new careers, it is equally important not to neglect the old standbys such as engineering, nursing, and teaching. A few years ago there was a great deal written about the fact that these areas are overcrowded and that one entering the field then would not be able to get a job. Soon after these pronouncements, came a series of articles on shortages in these fields, describing the extreme measures in which some communities are forced to engage to find qualified nurses and teachers. Both series of articles may have been true at the time they were written, but the lesson to be learned is not to believe predictions for the future when choosing a career. If you strongly want to be a teacher or a nurse or a member of some other field that is described as overcrowded don't be discouraged. Investigate for yourself. Become such a good member of that profession that you will be selected for the few positions that are available. You will then be well placed when the pendulum swings the other way and shortages appear. Don't be foolish about it, however. Certain professionals will always be needed but designers of buggy whips are less certain to be placed.

There are many sources you can use to find out about new careers. Don't neglect the closest at hand. Some may relate to a job you are presently performing or there may be a position in the company for which you presently work which you may desire. If you like your job but it does not offer you the money, security, or complexity you are looking for, is there a related field that might suit you for which you might train? For example, if you are a waiter or waitress would you like to remain in the food preparation area, but become a dietician or a chef? You can see how the thought process goes. If you are working for a large company, study the jobs posted by the personnel office. If the job requirements are not posted, talk to someone in the personnel office about what is required for positions which interest you. Remember that we are looking for a career, not just a job. Put these careers on the list you are starting.

70

Places to Search for Career Listings

There are many sources for creating this list of jobs. You could study the classified ads which appear not only in your local paper but also in such national papers as the *New York Times*. The Classified section of the *New York Times* is often not shipped around the country but a section with large display ads is usually available. These may be available in your library or you may be able to find them on-line on the

Internet. The phrase "on-line" is a key to the changes that have come about since my last book on careers. If you are persistent, it is possible to find practically anything you want on-line, that is, on the Internet. A later chapter will be devoted to finding information on the Internet which will be useful to your career search. If you do not have access to the Internet in your home, you may find a friend who will help you search or your local library may give you access to this incredible tool. We'll put together a list of queries designed especially for you so that you are not overwhelmed by the extent of the information you can find on the World Wide Web.

While computer searches are fast and exciting, don't neglect the old traditional methods of career search. Your public library or local high school may have a selection of materials on careers. College guidance departments can also provide such materials. Don't neglect the job listings posted on college and municipal placement boards or even in the "throw away" or shopper papers which are available in almost every community. Not only will these announcements give a job title and requirements, but they will most probably list a salary range. College catalogues can also be a source of ideas as you discover new majors that did not exist even a few years ago. Professional journals often list positions available in the field in the back of each issue. They may also have profiles of outstanding people in the field which lists their job titles. These individuals most probably do not hold entry level jobs, but remember you are looking at a career ladder. Their advanced position may be where your future lies in a few years. What kind of a career level does the entry level job lead to in that field? What are the tasks in these jobs? What requirements do you have to meet to get these jobs?

You may never have heard of these positions before. Some career ladders are not well known to the general public and may even be unknown to people on the beginning ladders of that career simply because they haven't investigated them. Many, but not all, of the new careers relate to technological developments.

If someone asked you to write down the titles of all the jobs that exist you would have an impossible task. New jobs would be created as you were trying to list the old ones. Some of the jobs would become obsolete or radically different even as you were

71

collecting information on them. Even if the search were limited to all jobs that you yourself could perform, the task would still be monumental because you would have to investigate the characteristics of a large number of jobs, some of which would be right for you and some of which would not be right at all.

The good news is that you won't have to conduct this search. Uncle Sam has done it for you and the information probably is available in your library and in a book you can purchase. And then there are the books which contain just lists of jobs. *The Dictionary of Occupational Titles* published by the U.S. Department of Labor lists thousands of jobs, many of which you probably have never even heard of.

The Occupational Outlook Handbook is published annually and may be obtained from the Bureau of Labor Statistics, Occupational Outlook Service, Washington, D.C. 20212.

Once upon a time, these books were owned only by certain libraries. Now both books have been made available in bookstores at reasonable prices.

72   The bad news about these books is that there are over 20,000 entries. If you have already chosen a new career area, I congratulate you. That's wonderful, but I would still like you to go through the listings. Although you may be quite certain of your selection, you will improve the odds for success in your career change if you do this review. Your selection may well stand up against all the other opportunities you review, increasing your certainty that you have chosen the right career, but you may also find something that is more interesting to you —something you never thought of before.

If you are like most people and are uncertain about which career to choose, the review will be absolutely necessary. Your knowledge of job areas and career ladders is limited by your experiences and possibly your reading. This listing will dramatically increase your knowledge of the "world of work," as it is still referred to by some high school counselors. In order to develop a list of possible careers you will have to match your abilities, interests, likes, dislikes, and limitations to the characteristics of a number of jobs. A number of characteristics accompany these listings. You do not have to learn the numbers of any of the categories in which you are interested but you will have to learn how the categorization works in order to make these materials most useful to you. The next chapter tells you very specifically exactly how these books are set up and can be used. It is recommended that you study Chapter Seven just before you review these books. They are a little difficult to understand in the abstract but much more easily understood if you have the books in front of you.

If you are unable to find these books in your local bookstore, they can be ordered for you or you can order them on line from such places as Amazon.com, Barnes and Nobles or Borders.

These books will give you not only information about specific careers but, *The Occupational Outlook Handbook* also presents some idea of the future of those careers themselves.

Looking at Agencies

State unemployment offices (or whatever they are now called in your state) may have a counseling center or at least a list of job openings in your geographical area. You do not have to be eligible for unemployment to use these agencies. Their listings are open to the public in most if not all states. In some places their job counselors are also available if you are a resident of that state. Call and find out and try to make an appointment that is convenient for you.

The personnel office of a company that interests you may also have job openings posted. City, county, and state agencies often will advertise jobs on bulletin boards by their personnel offices. It may be useful to fill out an application so that the municipality will have your information available and can send you announcements of jobs in your particular field. These announcements will often display salary and job qualifications while newspapers often do not give this information. With the competition for qualified personnel, the municipalities have to compete with salaries in the private sector. One of the positions you see listed may prove to be part of the "right" career ladder for you even if you are not yet eligible to apply for it.

Should You Hire a Career Counselor?

You may have wondered why I have not discussed the possibility of paying an individual to do this kind of analysis for you. The reason is that I sincerely believe you should do it yourself and this book is intended to help you through that process. You can be instructed to really investigate your potential and you know that you really care about the results. You may have seen advertisements encouraging you to visit a career counselor. This is one of the new careers that has developed over the past few years to assist people who are changing careers. The counselor is not responsible to help you find a new position and this fact is often not understood by the person who purchases the service. A good career counselor will take you through the same type of steps as this book. I recommend that you do this on your own unless you are very uncertain of yourself and your future. This is the case with many individuals. Sometimes, the services of a career counselor are offered by an employer as part of termination or outplacement. In that case, since it is free to you, take advantage of it, learn from it, but do not be bound by it. No one will know you better than yourself. As mentioned previously, some state unemployment agencies offer career counseling for free as well. Take advantage of everything you can get for free but be certain to place it in the context of your own instincts.

74

In view of the complexity of modern life and the number of career changes one can anticipate going through in a lifetime, it would seem that the profession of career counselor is a needed profession. The problem is that there is not a clearly defined body of knowledge which the counselor must have nor are there adequate licensing and consumer protection laws with regard to such activities.

Career counselors most often charge somebody a fee, whether it is private or a public agency, and sometimes these are very large fees. The career counselor may or may not administer certain placement type tests and may or may not be licensed to give you such tests. Some tests must be administered by licensed psychologists. The career counselors may or may not take you through the process we will be examining in this book. Some career counselors are excellent and will be an enormous help to you but others may do little more than talk to you about ideas you had when you entered their office or ones they continually propose to clients. If you use a career counselor, use the same standards as you would apply to any other professional. Be certain that his or her reputation is excellent, know what the service is going to cost you, have an advance agreement as to what you will get for your money and remember that abilities are different for different individuals. Local licensing laws vary and you might want to check into the requirements which are in affect in your area. Since you will have made a good study of career change before you finish this book, perhaps this would be a good career for you.

If your current position and/or career has fallen victim to technological advances or some other factor, you may be forced to find another career. Many companies are using the services of "outplacement" specialists. Outplacement means the process of letting someone be terminated while helping them to understand the reasons they were let go and to find a new direction for them to take in their career. The quality of outplacement firms varies. If your employer is offering this service, take advantage of it and participate fully in what it has to offer but don't depend totally on it.

In order to assist people in finding a career or taking the right courses, many colleges, especially community or junior colleges, and vocation schools offer testing programs as part of a counseling program. Many of these programs are excellent and you could not afford to take those tests as an individual. Some of these tests will be discussed in a later chapter. Do not think that the tests are silly when they ask you questions such as whether you would sooner spend the afternoon in the woods or go to an art show, or weather you would sooner be a forest ranger or an artist. The answers have been correlated over thousands of individuals. The only drawback is that many of the tests are old and do not take into account the demands of the age of technology. Again use your instincts with the results. A more specific discussion on testing will be given in a later chapter.

Remember that a career counselor or an outplacement specialist is not an employment agency and does not help you find a job. His or her role is to identify job areas which may be the "right" ones for you. I am not implying anything negative about career counseling agencies. They have a role to play, and some are excellent, but enter the process with caution and knowledge. I must admit that I personally believe in "do it yourself" when you can.

Employment Agencies as a Source of Career Ideas

Employment agencies must also be considered as sources of ideas for new careers. Employment agencies are in the business of matching people up with jobs but for the most part these agencies work for the employer. If you are considering a career change, you may be seeking counseling from the employment agency when that is not its role. Some agencies charge a large fee to the person seeking the job while others have the fee paid by the prospective employer. If you become involved with an employment agency, check its professional credentials and determine just what you will get for your money. Whether you pay the fee or the employer pays, check on the contract you will sign. What if the job doesn't work out either from your point of view or from the employer's? Who pays the fee then? I had a friend who took a job that turned out to be terrible but she still had to pay the fee once she accepted the position. She couldn't quit that job until she got the fee paid off and it was a substantial amount of money. Be clear on all the rules before you sign the contract. Check with the Better Business Bureau or its equivalent agency in your area to see if there have been any complaints filed against an employment agency you are considering using. Check with the courthouse to see if there are any cases filed against the employment agency.

Exercise 6.1

What outside help could you use to make your lists?

Make a list of the resources that you will use. This is an ongoing list of resources you will use or have used. It may include newspapers, professional career counseling, or books you are reading. Put on the list any resource that may be useful to you and used by you.

1._____
2._____
3._____
4._____
5._____
6._____
7._____
8._____
9._____
10._____

Self-assessment, counseling, and testing can all give you information to answer that important question: What new careers would interest you and be appropriate for you?

Do not limit yourself to old ideas and old concepts about careers. Look for something new. Think big. Think of something that will be exciting for you. Do not neglect opportunities with your current employer. Investigate all types of training programs with your company or with similar firms. Companies do not always expect you to be able to perform all aspects of a position when they hire you. You will have to demonstrate that you have the potential, but companies may be willing to place you in a program to develop that potential. Many companies have continuing education programs to train employees in areas that will be beneficial to the company. You may join a company in the job for which you are presently trained which will pay for your training in the field of your choice. They may also give you some time off to pursue the training. Some companies allow employees in a study program to leave early so as to get to evening classes or take some time off during the day. Others have programs on video or the internet which will offer the necessary training and credentials. Be imaginative about how you might fit into a company and how that company may help you attain your goals.

Some years ago, I visited the Johnson Space Center, in Houston, Texas. The place is fascinating, of course, but it was made so much more so by a young lady who served as our tour guide. She had an incredible amount of knowledge about the history of the space program and the performance of the various crews. She could describe in detail the history and use of the different components of the vehicles on display there. Since this is an active center, she was often asked questions about the projects people were currently working on as we passed or observed them from booths. She was able to give us some idea of the current projects at the center without going into extensive technical detail or revealing any top-secret material. When I asked her what she had done to prepare for this position, she told me she had been a secretary at the Johnson Space Center and had applied for the opening. NASA provided an excellent training program and she was always reading about the new developments to increase her knowledge. This young woman had made a very distinct career change using an opportunity within her own company and a training program they offered. She had the skills needed for the position. She was intelligent, interested in the space program, an excellent speaker, patient with questions and genuinely liked dealing with the people who came to NASA. An opportunity like this may not present itself to you, but do not neglect those that do come along.

Note that in the example above, I listed a few of the tour guide's characteristics that applied to her new job. If she were considering a career change, she might have made a list such as I have asked you to make. She would have included a great number of characteristics about herself and the kind of job she liked to do. Since she seemed to be such an organized, talented young lady, I would guess that her skills as a secretary were also good. Let us examine some of the characteristics of the new position which might be positive. She met many people. She talked about the space program. She was viewed as a knowledgeable person and respected by the individuals who came in contact with her. The subject about which she spoke was interesting and there were always new developments to add to her knowledge about the program.

Remember, however, there were also negative aspects to the position. The

78

Johnson Space Center is a very large complex and the displays are in many buildings. The tour guide is constantly on her feet, walking from one building to another with a large number of flights of stairs to be climbed on each tour. Some of this walking is between buildings that may not be too pleasant during Texas heatwaves or rainstorms. She has to dress well in order to make a professional appearance and there is a great deal of wear on her shoes and on her feet. She must always be ready to talk and answer questions. She has to be prepared. Not all visitors are nice. Some may want to go into restricted areas and may become difficult to control. She has to be "up" emotionally most of the time. I have no idea what her salary was but it probably was not much different than her salary as a secretary. When this young lady listed the positive and negative aspects of this job, the positive must have won by a large margin since she took the position and seems to be very happy in it. Some of the things which I list as negative, she (and you) may view as positive characteristics.

This is why it is important for each person to make his or her own set of lists relating to jobs. I can tell you how to do it, but I cannot make the judgments for you as to what you like or do not like. Or decide which career is the right one for you.

Data, People, Things

We can now consider one of the most useful aspects of these books. That is whether you are a person who is most interested in data, people. or things. Much of the classification of jobs is broken down into those categories.

Some of you may say I like all three areas but that is most unusual. I will give you a few examples so that you can relate your own interests. Accountants and computer programmers generally are more interested in data than the other areas. Engineers, manufacturers, medical researchers and repair people are generally more interested in things. Teachers, salesmen, comedians, and social workers are generally more interested in people.

The designation of these categories is not rigid and you will see later on in this book how they may vary. While you may immediately think you are most interested in one aspect, give it good consideration and be willing to change your mind as you consider alternative careers. At one of the book talks I have given, there was a very nice man who appeared to be undergoing a great deal of stress. Some time before, he had been a computer programmer working for a large firm but was a victim of cutbacks. Being at the difficult age of late forties with a young family, he had started his own business as a computer consultant. Starting your own business has been a successful option for many in the same position. In his business, he had to sell himself and what he could do for his clients, as well as introduce his product. He was fairly good at it and he could provide a reasonable living for his family, but he was very depressed As we talked, I came to realize that this man loved to work with data. Lock him in his office without a telephone all day, and he was a happy man, writing computer programs, solving problems. He became depressed only when he had to sell his product and deal with people. The development of relatively inexpensive software which allowed people to develop their own business plans and solve other business problems cut back on the products he could develop. The first solution which came to mind was for him to go back to a programming job in industry but these were still not readily available. It also was difficult to throw away the successful business he had built. The final solution was for him to find someone to do the selling for him, the people part, so that he could devote his time almost exclusively to the data part. This meant expanding his business so that it could support a second salary. His wife, who was a people person, would have been quite good at the selling role but she loved her job as a teacher and did not want to give that up. Finally he found a colleague of his wife who wanted to stay home with her children and was a good people person. She quickly understood the kinds of work he could do and because she probed the customers as to their problems expanded the product line beyond what the commercial software programs could handle. She worked primarily from her home in following up leads, quickly understood the kind of programs he could write, and got a baby-sitter for her children when she had to make a business call. His business was saved and two people had jobs at which they were happy.

80

Exercise 6.2

Are you most interested in data, people, or things? Really think about that answer. As we will see below, almost every career area can accommodate these different personality factors?

New Technologies / New Careers

The rapid rate of technological development and increases in the standard of living have combined to create a large number of new positions. The development of the computer, alone, has created a long list of positions which did not exist to any large extent except in a few research laboratories twenty-five years ago. With respect to computers, there are people who design them, make them, test them, program them, put groups of them together in a network, teach people how to make them, use them, fix them, run them, sell them and use them in one of thousands of applications. These are only some categories of computer-related positions. Within those categories are a number of different types of positions. In addition, computers touch on a number of seemingly independent careers. Medical technology, type setting, book design, architecture, dress designing and pattern making, for example, all rely heavily on computers.

Technology and increased services in the health-care field have combined to make this a very important area for new careers. Biomedical instrumentation has resulted in the development of amazing new instruments. Don't be frightened by the mention of medical technology, however. The gentle touch is still needed in the health-care field.

In spite of budget cutbacks, government work is still very attractive. At times it seems everyone works for the government but there are still a few openings. There are a number of very highly skilled positions opened in government work which are similar to those to be found in private industry. You do not have to be a member of a certain political party to get a government job (although in some cases that doesn't hurt). Civil service tests have taken a lot of the "good old boy" factor out of obtaining a government job. These jobs will vary once more as to their involvement with

81

data, people, and things.

Criminal justice is another area that has expanded rapidly. Bachelors and graduate level degree programs in criminal justice have certainly changed the field. Women as well as men are now selecting this area as a career opportunity. Forensics is an area that has developed rapidly with photographers, computer specialists, and scientists expanding that area.

Business is a complex area and there are many opportunities for those who are contemplating a career change. I have known a number of former teachers, for example, who have gone into the area of training and the development of training materials. These areas were related to teaching in a very broad sense but not in a specific sense. The former teachers needed some training themselves before they could make the change, but they have all enjoyed their new careers. Again, they were "people" people and were just focusing their old talents on new subject matter.

82

Using the Want Ads for Career Search

If you have identified a general area that interests you, search the magazines or journals which are written for people who work or study in that career, for the types of positions available. There are professional journals in almost every career area. Often they include articles on working in the specific career as well as problems and solutions to problems specific to the line of work. If you can't find them in your local library, try a college or university which offers that area as a major. Positions which are available are often advertised in those magazines or journals. You may not always get a lead as to the salary offered for a career which seems interesting, but you can track that down even if you have to answer an ad.

If your town is small, there may not be a great variety of careers or jobs listed in your local paper but, as previously discussed, it may be possible to get a copy of the New York Times, as well as some other newspapers from other major cities.

The *New York Times*, Sunday edition, like a number of other newspapers, has a section which lists many career-related positions in display ads as well as a section which has small classified ads. You may find a number of positions advertised here which are interesting and which you may never have considered before. Add those which seem interesting to your list.

You may know of positions which are too new to have been included in the books and magazines which you have read or in the general areas I have suggested above. Add them to your list as well. On the next pages, I have compiled a number of positions which I found listed in the classified sections of newspapers and in magazines and journals. These are but a small section from the types of positions being advertised in a number of geographic locations. You might find some listings of interest to you on these pages. There may be titles which you need to further investigate. Review your newspapers and college catalogs. Investigate interesting job titles and continue to add to your lists.

Hopefully, you will now have a pair of long lists to work with. Remember, the number one list is for special jobs and dreams. The number two list is for those occupations which didn't make it to the number one list but still have some appeal for you.

83

Making a Career Choice

The careers listed here are given in no particular order. Some are well known and well established while others are new. These positions are presented only to show you a range of possible careers. Perhaps there is something here which you can add to your own list.

84

FOREIGN BROADCAST SPECIALIST	GRAPHIC DISPLAY PROGRAMMERS
NATURALIST	AERODYNAMIC & PROPULSION ENGINEERS
MUSEUM INTERN	MICROPROCESSOR SYSTEMS ENGINEERS
REHABILITATIVE THERAPIST	PROGRAM MANAGERS
SPECIAL DELIVERY DRIVER	INSTRUCTORS IN TECHNOLOGICAL AREAS
DOCUMENTATION ENGINEER	PROJECT ADMINISTRATORS
FOOD TESTER	ANALOG/DIGITAL ENGINEERS
PHOTO-OPTICS TECHNICIAN	PRODUCTION PLANNER
BOTANIST	MECHANICAL DESIGN ENGINEERS
FOREIGN STUDENT ADVISOR	COMPUTER OPERATOR
WORK STUDY COORDINATOR	RECREATION DIRECTOR
CONTINUITY WRITER	CITY PLANNER
ARRANGER	ARCHITECTURAL DRAFTER
RACING SECRETARY	PRE-SCHOOL TEACHER
MIME	INTERIOR DESIGNER
ARBITRATOR	DANCE INSTRUCTOR
MANAGER OF CREDIT AND COLLECTION	PROGRAMMERS
PARKING ANALYST	TRAINING DIRECTOR
RADIATION MONITOR	SURVEYOR
CUTTER AND PASTER	CARDIOLOGIST
SATELLITE INSTRUCTION FACILITATOR	ACCOUNTANT
MAKE UP ARTIST	FIELD SERVICE ENGINEER
INSPECTOR	LAWYER
FISH ROE TECHNICIAN	INVENTORY CONTROL ENGINEER
POMPOM MAKER	PASTE-UP ARTIST
ELECTRONIC ORGAN TECHNICIAN	PHOTOGRAPHER
SCIENTIST	ADMINISTRATIVE ASSISTANT
TEACHER	FIELD SERVICE ENGINEER
SURGICAL ASSISTANT	PHARMACIST
BANKER	OPTOMETRIST
MORTGAGE BROKER	TRAVEL AGENT
CREDIT MANAGER	RESTAURANT MANAGEMENT
QUALITY CONTROL SUPERVISOR	HOTEL MANAGEMENT
PRODUCTION SUPERVISOR	REAL ESTATE MANAGEMENT
GROCERY STORE MANAGER	ENVIRONMENTAL ENGINEER
PERSONNEL COORDINATOR	DESIGN DRAFTER
RESPIRATORY THERAPY TECHNICIAN	ACTUARY
X-RAY TECHNOLOGIST	COMPTROLLER
MEDICAL TRANSCRIBER	WRITER
PHYSICAL THERAPIST	CONTRACT ADMINISTRATOR
PATIENT EDUCATION COORDINATOR	PUBLIC RELATIONS
LABORATORY PHLEBOTOMIST	JOURNALIST
SYSTEMS PROGRAMMERS	ADVERTISING
LABOR RELATIONS	PURCHASING AGENT
SYSTEM RESEARCH	ELECTRONIC TECHNOLOGIST
MARKETING	

It is indeed a crazy list but I wanted to impress on you the tremendous variety of positions that are identified from common sources.

Studying the Classifieds

If you are going to find the best new job as the first step in finding your new career you will have to learn to read the classifieds to find out what is being offered. Classified ads may be found in newspapers or they may be in magazines or journals related to a particular career.

Following are ads that have appeared in some papers.

85

> Test Engineer-Experienced engineer to engage in long-term test equipment design and build program. Practical experience is a must in the design and fabrication of digital analog test equipment. This position requires a degree with a minimum of three years experience.

If the ad says that they require a degree, you generally must already have the degree unless you are very close to graduation in a part-time degree program and have taken most if not all of the required courses in your major. The degree should be related to the job. A degree in English would not satisfy this requirement although you might get away with it if you had a great deal of experience and some education in the course work although you did not get a degree. You might be able to be a little short on the degree if you had good experience or a little short on experience if you had the degree, but you couldn't be both.

> Park Manager Graduate of accredited college with bachelor's degree in recreation administration or related field. Possession of degree in recreation administration or related field may be substituted for (1) year of required experience. Possess minimum (4) years responsible supervisory park management.

Hours spent in pick-up basketball games won't count here but there might be a combination of a degree in Business Administration with some activity in sports that would qualify you. The experience is very specific.

> Technical Instructors seeking professional instructors to instruct on installation and maintenance of XXXXX Systems. Trade school/industrial qualified telephone equipment instructor, telephone equipment installers or maintenance personnel preferred. Academically qualified teachers may be considered.

This ad gives a hint concerning how the basic requirements may be substituted by teaching credentials and experience in teaching in a totally different field. This is the way you must approach all job advertisements. What do I have that I might substitute for the listed requirement?

> Talented Writer—Your gift is needed for this public relations firm writing features and news stories.

This job apparently does not require either an educational background or experience. How could you show that you are a talented writer? By showing them your writing, of course. If you have published writing so much the better but your best writing may do. Make certain it is clean and neatly and accurately typed. Poetry may not be what they are looking for although it may show the creative mind they seek. Don't show them only your poetry. Make a portfolio, neatly arranged in a book with plastic sleeves, that demonstrates your range of writing abilities.

Now that you have the idea, see what could be done to modify the qualifications that are listed in the following ads so that a person with a different educational or work experience could handle the job. Does the ad itself contain some variations? Does it look like it would be an interesting job?

Data Entry —Expanding corporation has need for data entry operators. Will accept experience or will train good typist who would like to break into the data processing field. Pay commensurate with ability. Can lead to computer operator supervisor position for the right person.

Chief Flight Instructor —Local FAA approved flight school needs qualified chief flight instructor.

Paste - up Artist —To lay out newsletters and prepare charts for stock market advisory service.

Operating Funds Analyst—Bachelor's degree with a major in accounting, business or public administration and at least 2 yrs auditing ESP. either in private industry, public administration or public accounting. A master's degree in business or having successfully passed the CPA examination will substitute for 1 yr. of required work experience.

Personal Trust Administrator —Opportunity to join a winning team of results-oriented professionals in one of the fastest growing trust departments in the area. The ideal candidate will possess an undergraduate degree and a minimum of two years experience in all phases of personal trust account administration. If you are looking for a career position offering competitive pay, excellent benefits and exceptional growth opportunity. Send your resume to...

Scientific Programmer —This candidate will analyze scientific applications software written for XXXX in VVVV. Additional duties will be to design, code and document software for YYYY.

Material Control Coordinator —This candidate will direct and supervise the accounting, requisitioning and expenditures of all material and supplies required for the project. Several years experience in military supply or industry which deals with the military is required.

Technical Writer —Technical writers entry level and experienced to participate in the documentation of a new product. Knowledge of computer systems necessary.

87

Biologist —Assist in research on biological controls of aquatic weeds. Duties would include field and lab work, with aquatic insects and fauna, M.S. with major course in one of biological sciences or BS + 1 yr. biological work experience required.

Executive Director of Community-based Organization call...

Systems Programmer —Requires college degree in computer science and four (4) years experience in system's analysis, system and maintenance.

Pre-school Teacher —Needed to assist director and teach part-time

Senior Auditor —Currently seeking an individual interested in upward mobility and an opportunity to join a professional team involved in financial and operational audits. Qualifications include 3 to 5 years audit experience CPA, CIA or advanced degree and supervisory experience is helpful but not required.

Merchandising Assistant —Entry level position for busy catalog buying office. Excellent organizational skills, detail oriented, knowledge of Microsoft word and Excell. Good communications skills, ability to handle many projects at once. Retail Experience a plus. Fax resume to:

Office Manager XXXX Chevrolet —The world's largest volume Chevrolet Dealer seeks a motivated team player for busy, fast-paced office. Responsibilities to incl. a variety of office duties. Exp. in WP, Lotus & UCS helpful. Excellent benefits. No phone calls, please! Send resumes to...

Loan Officers —unique position with unlimited earning potential. License reqd.

Market Research —part-time good phone voice, organized, friendly for growing company. Retirees welcome starting $6.00 per hour.

88

You will see many ads like the last set as well as ads for telemarketing. Be careful. There are legitimate companies that do market research and telemarketing. In last Sunday's classified section our newspaper, itself, ran an ad for telemarketers. This was a legitimate ad, but there are many telemarketing companies that are sweatshops in the old meaning of the word and there are some that are running illegal operations. Also be careful of those ads which ask you to invest a certain amount of money to obtain a job or to buy products sold. If you work on commissions be careful to study the company very carefully. Check with the Better Business Bureau or equivalent. Check with the local board where employees can bring a complaint about not being paid. Have cases been successfully brought against this company? If you take the job, don't let the company get too far behind in paying you. Talk to other employees or the Better Business Bureau to see how frequently you will be paid your commissions and how far behind you will be in these payments. See if there are any claims before the local wage board or you might check with the police. While these are questions that you must ask at least in your own mind for every employer, it is particularly true in the telemarketing area. For most of these companies you must work in their shop, not at home. Be sure you determine the working conditions before you start. Be very careful when you take this type of job.

You have now reviewed a number of ads for positions. You know what to look for. Unfortunately not all ads are written well nor are they necessarily the best source for your new job. They are certainly one good source. Now you will have to decide what will be the first job in the career you have chosen.

You have reviewed many sources including books, ads, and professional publications, career counselors, and employment agencies. The next chapter will review the use of the *Dictionary of Occupational Titles* and *The Occupational Outlook Handbook* and then we will discuss in Chapter 8, our best tool for finding a career, the Internet.

89

Chapter 7

Using:
The Dictionary of Occupational Titles & The Occupational Outlook Handbook

The *Dictionary of Occupational Titles* and *The Occupational Outlook Handbook* were not designed for the use of ordinary people although they are quite effective used in that way.

The Department of Labor, during the massive unemployment of the depression years of the 1930's, tried to organize the titles and characteristics of all the jobs that existed. They created a system of numbers that identified many of the characteristics associated with different kinds of jobs. Jobs that are somewhat related are classified together. This information was first published in a large volume entitled the *Dictionary of Occupational Titles* in 1937. The successors to this first book are used by many, including the Unemployment agencies of the various states. Unless you ordered a copy from the government, it was formerly only available in libraries and in such places as state unemployment agencies. Now you can purchase a copy in your bookstore or over the internet at a not unreasonable price for the amount of information contained in it. The Dictionary will be invaluable for you, so find a comfortable location where you can use one for an extended period of time. While you don't need to own one, you will need a number of hours with it and you may need to copy some pages. Don't forget to bring some change with you for the copy machine if you are reading it at the library. As stated previously the classifications were developed to help the government get a handle on employment during the depression years of the nineteen thirties. There is a very strict formalism to the use of these books which must be followed although certainly not memorized.

In order to organize job categories, certain standard characteristics are used. For example, Standard Industrial Classification (S.I.C.) numbers were developed for use in the classification of establishments by the type of activity. Ten classifications are intended to cover the entire field of economic activities :

⇨ Agriculture, forestry, fishing, hunting, and trapping
⇨ Mining
⇨ Construction
⇨ Manufacturing
⇨ Transportation, communication, electric, gas, and sanitary services
⇨ Wholesale trade
⇨ Retail trade
⇨ Finance, insurance and real estate
⇨ Personal services, business services, repair services, and other services
⇨ Public Administration.

The inclusion of trapping and hunting in the first category gives you a clue as to how old and basic these classifications are. The mixing of communication, which is the largest growth area at the present time, with transportation comes from a time when the telegraph was the big means of communication. I don't know how it got coupled with sanitation. Even though this arrangement is obviously outdated, it is still useful.

The Dictionary of Occupational Titles (D.O.T.)has been updated a number of times. In the edition that was published in 1949, there were 17,500 entries. The 1960's represented a period when a number of new types of jobs were created by technology and there was a major increase in the number of entries. A substantial effort was made in the 1970's to reduce the number of entries by eliminating those which are generally "out of date." The 4th edition, which was printed in 1977, contains approximately 20,000 jobs. The return to basic living and arts and crafts required that some of these deleted entries be reinstated along with the development of new technologically based jobs. The latest revisions include a number of jobs in the technical area.

Considering the number of entries, the odds are in your favor that the perfect career for you is listed in the Dictionary of Occupational Titles. Since I have just told you the number of entries, I can see you sitting there saying "She isn't going to ask me to read all of those entries and make lists from them, is she?"

Of course I am, but with a lot of limitations! You will have some other tasks to do first. If you follow the steps outlined below, this search will either confirm that you have selected the right career, or it will introduce you to some other interesting options.

The Dictionary has an excellent section in the front of the book which describes its use. In the back of the book is a small section which describes some of the philosophy underlying the book. In order to use the book most effectively, you must relate this philosophy to your own life. Although the book is often used only to classify titles, the items include many pieces of information about each job which is classified using a coding system. The first digit of the general code number for the listing specifies the occupational group.

The third edition of the D.O.T. lists the following as the key to the first digit in the number. Both 0 and 1 are used for the first category.

0/1 Professional technical and managerial occupations

2 Clerical and sales occupations

3 Service occupations

4 Farming, fishery, forestry and related occupations

5 Processing occupations

6 Machine trades occupations

7 Bench work occupations

8 Structural work occupations

9 Miscellaneous occupations

These ten groups are then broken down into eighty-four, two-digit divisions and the divisions, in turn, are subdivided into 603 distinctive three-digit groups. These groups form the basis for the second and third number in the job number code.

The fourth, fifth and sixth numbers are somewhat subjective. As indicated in the fourth edition on page 1369, each job title is related to the degree in which the worker is expected to function in relation to three areas: data, people and things. Only "occupationally significant" relationships are indicated, since every person, in every job must be able to function in a general manner to each of these areas.

These headings play such a significant role in the designation of the job title that they are represented by the fourth, fifth and sixth digits of the occupational code numbers. The highest value in each of the columns in table 1 is selected for representation in the job number.

94

DATA (4th digit)
0 Synthesizing
1 Coordinating
2 Analyzing
3 Compiling
4 Computing
5 Copying
6 Comparing

THINGS (6th digit)
0 Setting-up
1 Precision Working
2 Operating-Controlling
3 Driving-Operating
4 Manipulating
5 Tending
6 Feeding-Offbearing
7 Handling

PEOPLE (5th digit)
0 Mentoring
1 Negotiating
2 Instructing
3 Supervising
4 Diverting
5 Persuading
6 Speaking-Signaling
7 Serving
8 Taking Instructions-Helping

Before you can identify your standing on these characteristics, you must know what they mean. The definitions as used by the Department of Labor in their coding are given in Appendix A. The department's definitions may not be your definitions and they certainly aren't the first definitions that come to my mind. They may not seem to be complete or they may seem to allow too much overlap. Whatever your judgment, they are the key to the numbers assigned to various jobs and they will help you to identify the various components of positions so that you do not have to study the full 20,000 entries in the same detail. Many of them you will be able to skip entirely.

The ratings from 0 to 6, 7 or 8 are not judgments of the value of the items. A job that involves a 0, to a much larger extent than any other number, is not a better or a worse job, but a different job. The list has been arranged in order of complexity with the more difficult component including the simpler elements. Please read and reread the explanation, if necessary.

If you have decided to skip over the pages which have been reprinted from the Dictionary of Occupational Titles, please go to the appendix and look at them. If you find some of the phrasing difficult and/or unclear, please reread those items. Changing your life is hard work. You don't have to memorize anything but deciding whether you are most oriented to data, persons, or things is a significant key to your choosing a career.

We will use these definitions as a starting point for an analysis of your likes and dislikes with respect to job tasks. These, in turn, will form part of the basis for identifying the characteristics of a new career. The next step will be the identification of the restrictions on the position. The final step will be selection of the career itself. Now, it is time to get out the paper and pencil again.

Finding a Job in the *Dictionary of Occupational Titles*

Almost all positions involve working with the three basis elements of data, people and things but most focus on one of these elements to a much larger degree than the others.

Exercise 7.1

If you had to select data, people, or things as the primary focus for your new position which would it be?

_____

Exercise 7.2

Which characteristic would be second? Would it be a close second or would it miss by a great deal? Which one would be third?

_____

Exercise 7.3

Would it be tolerable or would it be dreadful if the new position contained a great deal of that element? Some people hate working with numbers, other people love it. Some people do not like a great deal of interaction with people. Other people are afraid of or are repelled by machines. To each his or her own, but know what your own is.

Remember this part of the analysis when you are selecting jobs to review in greater depth. The fourth digit of the code number for the job identifies the highest component of data. The fifth digit of the code number identifies the highest component of people and the sixth digit of the code number identifies the highest component of things. Look for those items which include the functions you like in the more complex form and look for the functions you don't like in the simplest form and with the least emphasis. As examples, 000601000 will be high in data, low in people and machines, while 000161000 will be high in people, low in data and machines. If you don't want to be bothered with all of this number business, just think of data, people, things as components of any jobs you are considering.

Notice as you study the definitions of the Worker Functions how they can vary within the same category. Under people you have a broad variety of choices. A "2" might be attached to a teaching type position while a "4" might go with an entertainment role and a "5" might accompany a salesperson's position. A person who would make an excellent teacher might be a terrible salesperson even though he or she would have to interact with people in each position. On the other hand, the same person might be good in all three roles but in most cases will prefer one of them.

Many positions are not completely clean with respect to the worker functions. You can translate that as "life is not simple." But the process still is valid and valuable. Write down the numbers under each of the digit headings which would interest you

96

and write down those which would be a no-no. There is no point in looking at entries which would involve components which you couldn't stand.

After you have conducted this analysis, you are still faced with the prospect of going through the 20,000 entries. The task will be lightened, however, by the way in which the entries are grouped. Don't just plow into the book. Study the categories of entries, they are grouped together in very useful ways. For example, if you have always been interested in biology, you will find several very different types of positions under general headings that involve the word biology. The indexes offer different ways to find related entries. You will be able to eliminate many, many listings through their indexed heading by the code number or by the first few words of introduction.

A substantial amount of renumbering occurred from the third edition (1965) to the fourth edition. This is shown in the following list of examples of entries from the Dictionary. Some of the titles were chosen to show you the variety of jobs which are classified. Study the examples before you begin your work so that you will have a good understanding of the design of the entries.

97

JOB TITLE	3rd edition	4th edition
Perfumer	022.181-014	022.161 -018
Poising Inspector	715.387-022	715.384-018
Poet	130.088-022	130.067-042
Pocketed-spring inspector	780.887-046	780.684-050
Secretary	201.368-018	201.362-030
Seamstress	782.884-078	787.682-030
Teacher, nursery school	359.878-026	359.677-018
Teacher, art	149.028-010	149.021-010
Teacher, technical ed.	090.228-026	090.227-010
Telephone operator	235.862-026	235.662-022
Pony ride operator	349,228-010	349.224-010

Do you know what a poising inspector inspects? As an exercise in learning to use the Dictionary try looking up the entry for poising inspector. There are many interesting listings in this book you can explore. Note how many of the rating numbers changed. Pay special attention to the fourth, fifth and sixth digits.

Bring filecards with you and jot down such information as code number, job title, pertinent characteristics and page number in the D.O.T. For those entries which seem to be most interesting, be a big spender and make a photocopy of the page using the copy machine which can be found in most libraries. Bring change because they often do not have the facility for making change. Your time is more important than the little bit of money that is involved. After all, you are planning your future and you will want to review this information after you leave the place where you are studying the D.O.T. You might even invest a modest amount of money in one of the new paperback copies of the D.O.T.

What new ideas did you get from this book? Remember not to eliminate those ideas that really appeal to you but for which you do not have the training. We will work on ways for you to get that training later. Make these additions to your class one and class two lists of possible careers. Did you find a lot of new things to add to your lists? Were some of these jobs ones you did not think about before? Were some of these careers ones you had never even heard of before? What made them seem interesting to you?.

Following Trends in the *Dictionary of Occupational Titles*

In spite of the fact that there are so many entries in the *Dictionary of Occupational Titles*, there may be jobs that you have thought of but which have not been listed or which may not have been listed as being attractive. A number of entries considered to be outdated were removed in this edition and a substantial number of new entries were added.

Some of these positions may not be out of date with respect to what you want to do. I haven't looked to see what the *Dictionary of Occupational Titles* has to say about the manufacture of buggy whips but I would venture a guess that it is not listed anymore, if it ever was. Many careers which are related to the making of handmade products are not necessarily out of date any more. Many crafts that were once considered to be only profitable in terms of pleasure are now producing good incomes for their practitioners. If your interests lie in this area however, you will probably not find these listed in any general catalog, but you will have to look in specialized magazines to discover your opportunities. You will also have to consider operating your own business. This is discussed in a later chapter. Add these things to your lists, if they interest you.

A number of career areas project an increase in positions in the next few years. *The Occupational Outlook Handbook* not only discusses new careers but also attempts to project the future of those careers. You may find a career there that you can begin to prepare for now.

Chapter 8
Using the Internet to Find a Career

The acceptance of the internet has been accomplished with phenomenal speed. A few years ago, the internet was used only by technical types. Now the stereotypes are gone with regard to who uses the internet. Age limits have faded, especially with regard to electronic mail more commonly known as e-mail. Grandparents who would have scoffed at anyone saying they would have an interest in using a computer only a year or two ago are are sending and receiving messages and photographs from their children and grandchildren. People write to friends in foreign countries on a regular basis. I would commonly write to my cousin and her family in England two or three times a year and would receive an answer back from her at the same rate. Now we use e-mail to keep in touch. In one six week period we exchanged letters six times. They weren't long letters and they might have only said something like "we were eating your favorite kind of bagel this morning and couldn't help but remember the good time we had at breakfast the morning before you left." Not very profound but a very human link. And our long distance phone bill has also reflected the increased use of the Internet.

But what is the Internet? The internet is a network of networks. It is not owned by any one person or by any single company. It is not maintained by any individual or company either but by thousands of contributors who have integrated themselves into this massive network. There are certain rules which have been established by the participants such as a rule with regard to the uniqueness of addresses but the rules are very few and only relate to the minimum functioning of the system.

In order to use the internet you have to have certain software known as a browser and you have to link with a network provider or use some alternate method. You might update your telephone system with a DSL line or use a digital line through your cable network. Change in this area is being made so quickly that there will undoubtedly be another method by the time this book is printed.

In addition, the Internet is invaluable for searching for information. As a person choosing a career, that should perk your ears up. Information forms the basis for your choice of career and the Internet will permit you to get massive amounts of information without leaving your office, your bedroom or wherever you choose to set up your computer system. Those ads which show users in their bathrobes searching the net at all times of the day and night are not just trying to induce you to join the masses of people using the internet. They are showing you the true state of internet use for many subscribers. I often get up early to write and you'd find me in my nightgown at my computer if you came to my house early enough.

In order to use the internet with a computer, you have to have a modem or other device which will allow you to transmit and receive over telephone lines or use a cable connection. You must then enter into an agreement with a service provider who will provide the connection that is required to hook your computer up to the internet through your telephone lines. If you are in a populated area, you should be able to find a provider who will give you a local number to dial your connection to the Internet. If you are going to sign up with a provider, check with friends for recommendations. Don't necessarily go with one who is going to give you a reward, such as a camera or cash back. Go with one that will give you good service. When you want to get on-line, you don't want to have to keep dialing back to get a connection. You want to get on-line right away. You don't want a busy signal or be required to make your connection at some odd hour in order to get through. It is like choosing a doctor, dentist or lawyer. You can't beat a good recommendation from a friend.

You will then need software that is called a browser. Much of the Microsoft anti-trust controversy was focused on the sale and use of browsers. If you are choosing this type software, have a friend or your favorite computer store recommend software that will allow you to connect in the simplest fashion. You most probably will not need to have your own home page in the beginning although you may move into that option fairly quickly. If you start your own business, whether it is an e-business, that is a business which functions on the Internet, or not, you will need to do some advertising on the Internet which will require your own homepage. That will be discussed further in the chapter on starting your own business.

There is another possibility for connecting to the internet. This is through your television. One of the product lines for doing this is known as Direct TV. For someone who does not feel the necessity of owning a computer, purchase of a Direct TV box may be an ideal solution. There are some restrictions with regard to the characteristics of the television you may use with this box but almost any modern television set should meet these requirements. You will also need a telephone connection. Depending on where you live, the call you make to your service company should be a local call. This is what makes e-mail so economical. The fact that you are communicating with someone in a far distant state or country does not cause you to be billed for a long distance call. You may also access the internet with your computer or Direct TV when you travel but you may be charged for long distance calls to the number you use at home for your service provider in that instance. Some providers will make arrangements for you to "travel" with your computer for a small daily charge. Check all of these charges with your service provider or Direct TV provider when you sign up for the service. You should also determine how long a time period your agreement will cover. If you do not get good service from your provider, you do not want to be locked in for a long period of time.

Just as when you are making a phone call from a foreign country, and have to use country codes and area codes as well as the number, there are various components to the e-name which you must include. Be certain to get all of the components from the person who is giving you their address when you are just starting to get

103

familiar with using the Internet. Don't let them assume you know all of the codes which must be entered or all of the symbols. After you have done it a few times, it will be easier for you.

Addresses almost always must be entered in lower case letters with no spaces in between. Using capitals or spaces is the source of much frustration in sending mail and having it come back as unable to be delivered.This book will not go into the structure of names. The only secret is to "get them correct".

In addition to using e-mail, you can also do searches for information. Your browser will allow you to access various search engines. These are companies that have created databases you can access to get information. This may be general information or it may be very specific. Let me give you an example. One of the places I was going to visit on my trip to Ireland in June, 2000 was a place in County Cork known as Baltimore. There was to be a gathering of the Driscoll clan of which I am a member through my mother's family. I wanted to reserve a room in Baltimore for myself and my husband. Since I knew the town was quite small and would be crowded with the clan gathering, I did not want to wait until we got there to find a place to stay. One night, I searched the term "Baltimore, Ireland" and found information on the clan gathering and the bed and breakfasts that rented in Baltimore. I sent e-mails to six of them and received answers back from five of them. Only one had an opening, I booked with her and sent her a deposit by mail. Without the Internet I could not have done it. It was, by the way, a lovely place to stay with a gracious hostess and we would definitely return there.

You can also buy and sell things over the Internet. My daughter just purchased new skis at a large discount from a store in Colorado which had an overstock and our son has bought things related to his interest in Rugby and cycling which he could not find elsewhere. e-Bay is one site which currently does this. Both stores and individuals use these sites for buying and selling. You are taking a chance on the quality of the merchandise. If you sell something, you must make certain the check is not only in the mail but will clear before you ship the merchandise. It is another source of entertainment but like everything else, understand what the risks are before before you get involved.

You can also search for your family's roots on the Internet. This is especially valuable when jointed with some of the software packages that are available for doing this. I bought my husband a program that has 75 computer discs containing information on immigration including passenger lists on the ships that carried the immigrants from many different countries to different ports in the United States. The program also provides links or connections to many different search engines so that more extensive searches can be performed.

As you can see from the above examples, in addition to e-mail, the Internet provides access to endless amounts of information. This is not just the type of information you would find in a good encyclopedia but very detailed information about unusual topics. Using the search engine you have selected, you do a search using the rules of that search engine to connect words. The more effort you take with selecting the right words for your search, the more precise your answers will be. For example, if I had only entered the word "Baltimore" instead of "Baltimore, Ireland" I would have gotten information about Baltimore, MD as well as Baltimore, Ireland and information about other entities that contained the word Baltimore in their title like Baltimore and Ohio Railroad. The more limitations you put on your search, the narrower it will be and the more useful it will be. It is discouraging to get no information but it is also discouraging to see that your query resulted in fifty thousand hits or even five thousand hits. Even if you do get a large number of hits, begin to review the ones in the beginning of the list to see if you are at least on the right track in your search.

A homepage is a site developed by or for the person who owns the homepage. It may be a company or an individual. Many writers have their own homepage to let their readers know such information as when their latest books are coming out and where they will be doing book signings.

Using the internet, you can go to the homepages of colleges and universities which might either interest you as a place to attend or be a place which might have information about new areas of study. Most, if not all, colleges and universities have their catalogues on line and you can research them for much valuable information.

You may even be able to apply for admission to the college on-line, that is by filling in an application form on the computer by answering questions that will be asked on-line. Not only can you get class schedules, costs and admission standards, but you can find information about the latest programs developed by the institution. This may point you in the direction of careers which you have never thought about.

If you find the web sites for companies in which you are interested, many of them will display personnel openings and may even include salary. Some companies allow you to fill out an application on the computer and submit it electronically. Others request you to send a resume by e-mail. The more technically oriented the company, the more information you will find on-line although almost every company is represented to some degree.

You may also find information about employment agencies and career counseling agencies but remember that they prepared the information and are certainly "biased" in their appraisal of their abilities to find you the employment you desire.

106   The following are examples of a few Web sites and searches I have carried out to give you an idea of how it is done. I am not necessarily recommending these sites or careers. They are simply sites that I found to be useful but there are hundreds more out there that you can work with. Remember with the daily changes in technology some of these sites may have been closed when you try to use them. Don't let that discourage you. A dozen others have probably taken their place. Don't neglect this powerful new tool.   Don't be afraid of it.

An interesting and very useful website is called monster.com. It accepts resumes from job applicants as well as posting job openings from employers. It may try to match prospective employers and employees. It also gives many hints about such topics as writing a resume or presenting yourself at a job interview. There are examples of such documents as inquiry letters and resumes on which you can base your own efforts in addition to what is included in a later chapter in this book. Plan to spend several hours using this website if you are going to take full advantage of everything it has available. And, as with the use of many websites, there is no charge for its use. Don't think you are going to do all of your searching for information on new careers at one sitting.

Chapter 9

Making a List, Checking It Twice

Ridicule can be more effective than any knife to slice apart a dream. Have you ever had that happen to you? Have you ever given up on a dream because of what others said about it? Are there any old dreams left on any of your lists of possible careers? Are there any survivors of sharp-tongued ridicule? Keep them—nurture them–they may not be impossible to achieve. They will have to be studied and protected until you are able to defend them.

There are many individuals who have had the courage and have taken the opportunity to follow a career or career change in their lives. In this chapter we will discuss some ways to accomplish this and we will look at some individuals who have done this. First, we have to find the right career for you. It may be that old dream and then again, it may not.

Using the List to Find the Right Career

You want to make a change in your life. You want people to stop asking you what you are going to do when you finish college or what you are going to do with the rest of your life. Do you want to make this decision for the sake of change or is the selection of a new career very important to you? There is nothing wrong with wanting some change and selecting your career to be its focus. In this case, however, you must realize the change in career may not bring about the change in your life which you desire. Study the question of change very carefully. How much can you expect from your new career?

You cannot consider a career selection in isolation. Your career takes up a large part of your life. Let us assume you have twenty-five years left of career productivity and let us assume you work an eight-hour day. Many executives and professionals work more like a sixty-hour week than a forty-hour week but we'll settle for the lower figure. Now let us assume you get five weeks of vacation and assorted holidays. That means you will be working 25 x 47 x 40 =7,000 hours. That is a long time to be unhappy in a job. Remember that just changing jobs may not solve your problem if the problem is not initially job related. If you have more years than the twenty five of work, the example above should be changed to reflect the additional time.

If you are certain you want a new career, you must then consider all the steps involved in the change as being very important to you. Every step is part of the link in the chain. There are not too many shortcuts you can take. Attaining a new career will not be simple. It will demand a great deal from you and from your family. You must be certain that the new career is the right thing for you. How do we find the right one? Back to the lists!

You have racked your brain, probed your soul, analyzed a book with 20,000 entries, developed lists, reviewed your lists, read thousands of entries in the Dictionary of Occupational Titles, read newspapers, professional magazines and journals from everywhere and who knows what else. The product of all your work is, hopefully, a list or lists of careers that appeal to you.

Now that you have created all of these lists what do you do with them? Why, you break them up into smaller lists! You now have a number of career areas on at least two different lists. Make each of these careers titles the heading of a new page.

Under each career heading, list

1. Your abilities which support that career area. Include potential that could be developed through training or education.

2. The characteristics associated with the career that either match items on the

"good job characteristics" list you made before, or are positive ones that you have identified from reading about the career or by talking with someone who is already in that position.

3. The characteristics of the career that are on the "bad job characteristics" list you made before or which might seem to be bad. Again, the fruits of your research.

4. The things you would have to do in order to prepare for that job. Include, for example, going back to school, moving, or borrowing money to study or start a business.

5. The anticipated reaction to this career from those whom you care about.

6. An estimate of the odds on your getting a job in that career field at your age and with your work background and talents. This is perhaps the most difficult factor to project, but you must do it realistically. You may need to talk to someone in this field or an employment counselor in order to make a realistic appraisal of your future in this field.

7. A complete description of what the job is really like. In order to do this you may have to talk to people who have that job. Although it is sometimes difficult to find people in a particular career in your geographic area, it is important to find out just what a job is really like. What appears to be a glamorous occupation as described in a pamphlet, may really have some aspects which will not appeal to you at all. What are the day-to day tasks? What are the opportunities for advancement? Find out before you make the change. You may have to do your searching for answers by telephone if you cannot accomplish this in person.

8. The beginning salary for this career. What kind of increases could you expect? How long would it take to move up in this field? Note that I inquired about the starting salary. You may be able to get more than the starting salary because of your past experience but don't depend on it. Inflation has done strange things with salaries. Beginning salaries have had to be raised to keep up with inflation but longevity increases don't even seem to be keeping up with beginning salaries and non-relevant experience is not always considered in placing you on the salary scale. Can you live on this income? Is it better or worse than what you have available to you now? If you

have to make a financial investment for study or a geographic move, will you be getting a good return on your money? Is this an important consideration for you?

9. Are you suffering from boredom at the present time? Are there repetitious elements to the new job or first job in a career ladder with which you may become bored in a short time?

10. What kind of feelings will the new career cause you to have? Pride, excitement, fear . . . what will these emotions be? Will you increase your positive feelings toward yourself? Will others increase their positive feelings toward you?

11. Would you estimate that changing to this career would accomplish for you some of the things that are most important for you?

12. The answers to any other questions which you have identified as important but which I have not included above. Do this kind of evaluation for all the careers that you have written down.

Are there any careers that you can definitely eliminate at this point? Do not use the criteria of education or cost as a basis for elimination but you may use the other criteria, such as: the job is too hard to get, the starting salary is too low, there are too many boring tasks, etc.

Take all of yours sheets now and once more make a list of the careers that are left. This will be your next to the last working list unless you have now crossed everything out and have to start over! In the next Chapter, I will ask you to do a set of calculations that will help you evaluate all of these lists.

Now that you have all these lists, what will you do next? At some point you have to stop making lists and make a choice of the new career! This will be easier if you can project some plans for attaining your goal. Please, please don't scrap those old dreams. Don't let anyone else's ridicule change your mind.

Changing careers, going back to school, and following dreams, both old and new, have become more readily acceptable in recent years. I have only to look around me to give you some examples of people doing this very thing. If you feel that I am telling your story, I probably am (and I am very proud of you). I changed careers myself, from being a college administrator to being a lawyer. There are important characteristics of each of those careers that meet my emotional needs even though the job tasks are very different.

Success Stories

An engineer I know entered medical school in his early forties, at considerable sacrifice to himself and his family. He is an excellent doctor in a large city and has long ago demonstrated just what a good idea this was.

A young black woman who had a fifteen-year career in art management (museums, galleries) also went to medical school. This had been an early dream of hers but she was discouraged in reaching this dream by high school guidance counselors. She went to medical school with the emotional and financial support of her family and today has a successful practice.

An airline pilot with a number of auxiliary interests including sailing, began to paint somewhat late in his very active working life and found he had tremendous talent and a growing market for his watercolors. He has phased in this new career on a gradual basis and is now making a very fine living from it. He also derives a great deal of pleasure from his new occupation which will carry him through what would normally be his retirement years. He teaches classes in watercolor and has recently written some books and produced videos about his painting techniques. His articles have appeared in national magazines. Again he has a wonderful, supportive wife who has helped him along the way and become a well known potter and teacher of pottery herself while he developed his watercolor skills.

A teacher I know became a successful textbook author. Not only is he an extremely wealthy man as a result, but he has done a great deal to make a difficult subject interesting and to humanize the curriculum in his field. He never thought that this would happen when he spent those long hours writing that first book each day after school.

111

Family support was obvious in the case of the wife of a prominent local man. Her enrollment in law school was followed closely by that of two of her children. All three have had a successful experience. Mother and son are already practicing and daughter will graduate next June.

A gentleman who has reached the limits of opportunity within industry because of the lack of a degree has returned to school on a part-time basis to get a degree in electrical engineering. His son is enrolled in a similar program in another school. Combined with the practical experience he already has, the degree will open up a number of different job advancements for him. In addition, his present employer is paying for a substantial part of his educational expenses.

A widow with ten children, some of them grown, who had worked as a teacher aide for a number of years, returned to school and obtained her own teaching degree. It was a matter of pride, not only for herself, but for members of her family as she was an example, not only to her own children but to her nieces and nephews.

An elementary school teacher, who began taking singing lessons as courses toward the renewal of her teaching certificate, was encouraged by her teacher after only a year of lessons to enter a competition against people who had been studying for years. She won and thus began a second career of opera singer in addition to her regular teaching position. Within the first few years of her career, she had an opportunity to sing a small part in an opera with Pavarotti! This was a dream she never thought she could fulfill, but she did. Don't give up on your dreams, no matter how foolish they may seem.

Another teacher who went to a community college for a degree in mortuary science found that he could complete the program in a year because of his previous work. He carried out this second occupation on the weekends by being on call at a number of funeral homes for emergency replacement of their regular staff. He eventually was able to purchase a small funeral home himself. his people skills were of great use in comforting the bereaved.

A woman who was tired of office work opened a consignment shop for children's clothes. She has just expanded her shop by renting space next to the bay she occupies.

Not everything has gone perfectly for everyone. Some succeed, some fail. Those who tried, however, at least followed their dreams and that was important to them. Not trying is the greatest failure.

The family plays an important positive role in many of the successful stories related above. It is not only a matter of the family allowing you to change your career. It is a matter of the family participating in that career change and supporting you when you are down emotionally or financially.

The examples I have given above are of people changing careers. Although it is often easier to start a career when you are young, this is not always the case. The people in the stories above had an income while they moved into the new career. All of the difficulties you have when you are young are repeated when you are older plus you have all the needs of supporting a family while training for the new job and the problems of getting a job in any area when you are older.

113

Steps to Take

If you are going to build the scheme for moving to a new career, you will have to take the following steps.

1. Identify the new career which you would like to enter.

2. Research all aspects of this career.

3. Identify your strengths and weaknesses with respect to this career.

4. Involve your family in the process of considering the new career.

5. Obtain the additional education or training needed to enter the new field if necessary.

6. Prepare the image necessary for you to enter the new career.

7. DO IT.

Always keep this new goal in proper perspective. Your career is only a part of your life, an important part, indeed, but still only a part.

The "scheme" is very straightforward. If the new career seems to be the right one for you, taking everything into account, then you must make the necessary sacrifices to achieve the career change.

You will have to make plans, work hard, sacrifice perhaps, take chances, do what you must do to obtain it, but DO IT.

Chapter 10

Sidelines

For those who are not able to commit themselves to a career change, the option of a sideline is often a viable alternative.

Moonlighting Your Way to a New Career

Moonlight and dreams go together and this is especially true in the case of achieving your new career. Moonlighting is the name often given to the activity of those who supplement their regular work with additional employment in an area which may be different from their main position. A second job may be the answer to your career dilemmas.

You may choose a career area for a number of reasons. One may be that the area will give you greater financial security than the previously held career. At times a person may really be selecting a career, as opposed to a job, for the first time in his or her life. Many times the career the person dreams of entering is one in which it is difficult to get a position. It may be that the person could get a position in the new field, but could not make an adequate living in that position.

I would love to write or paint for a living, but it would be many years before I could even begin to generate an income from that activity equal to that which I earn in my present career of law. It would be a risk for me to give up my regular position and write full time. In addition, I like my present career. Until I feel that the time is right, I will "moonlight" and continue to write early mornings, after work and on the weekends and paint and take photographs when I can. It certainly is not the best way to improve my writing and artistic skill but it is a compromise which allows me to meet both the goal of financial survival and artistic satisfaction.

My friend, the pilot, who is now a successful painter on a full-time basis, maintained his other position and painted part time until his talent developed and his income rose to a sufficient level to support him. He no longer flies now, except for pleasure, and is able to paint and teach painting full time. He has done a number of articles, videos and books about watercolor and painting boats. His wife became a full time potter and teaches that art as well.

Remember the friend of mine who was a teacher and was also a part-time mortician. He kept the security he had as a teacher for several years while building his second career. He finally retired from teaching and opened his own funeral home. First he got the licenses he needed and built up his experience. He also became certain that he really wanted the new career, which was radically different from his old one.

A policeman I know who needed the security of a regular position to support his large family, does fine carpentry work and remodels kitchens on weekends in the small town in which he lives. He gets a great deal of satisfaction from it as well as a steady supplement to his regular income. He could not begin to replace the benefits his large family enjoys if he only did his carpentry work and he is a policeman in a town which has a low level of violent crime. He also enjoys people which he would not be able to do if he isolated himself in his carpentry shop.

A number of people work as consultants in a specific field while retaining their original positions. Another teacher friend will retire after thirty years in the school system and begin a MFA in writing. He has been an actor in local promotions for many years. Some people have an excellent second career already established when they take early retirements from their first careers. This is important for those who may receive a pension after fifteen or twenty years of work in a specific area . Those who work as police or firemen often have this opportunity. Some school districts may also offer retirement after a certain number of years. These individuals are often too young to sit home or just play golf and they often are restricted by their pension from working in the same area or for the same government employer.

Individuals who retire from the military often find themselves in the position of needing to develop a second career area. Some service areas provide excellent preparation for a career in the business world. Some military and private sector areas are almost identical and full credit for experience may be given. Other areas, however, are quite unique to the service and the person seeking the second career may have trouble identifying transfer possibilities. The service offers many opportunities for schooling and some individuals prepare themselves for life after retirement from the military while still in uniform. They may begin to follow a new career as a hobby or sideline while still in the service.

Those who are working in a technical field or in a vocational area may want to teach in that field. This isn't as simple a matter as it may appear at first. In order to teach in the public schools in most states, you must have a teaching license. To obtain this license you must complete specific courses as well as a practice teaching program during which time you teach under the supervision of a licensed teacher. Most colleges will not allow you to come into their program for only a few courses and then do practice teaching. You may find that you have to take an extensive program first. The rules concerning licensing are somewhat different in vocational schools but they still require specific academic preparation. Having a license to teach in one state does not mean you can automatically obtain a license in another state. These will all be things you will have to look into with regard to specific rules for the community in which you desire to teach.

Teaching, however, is a career which can be done on a part-time basis. Many vocational schools have evening programs that use teachers who are experienced in a particular field. These evening schools do not have the same rigid rules for teaching as do the daytime vocational schools. You might also try to get a license

117

that allows you to substitute in a school. This means you would fill in for a teacher who is out for a specific period of time. It might be because he or she woke up with the flu or is on leave due to an illness. Substitute teaching could give you an opportunity to discover if you would like to teach before you have made a full commitment to it. You can often substitute teach before you have met all of the licensing requirements to teach in a particular community. Remember that substitute teachers are paid much less than regular teachers in a school system and do not develop the bonds with students when they are sent to different schools every day to teach.

As mentioned above, another setting in which you can teach is in adult education programs. If you fear you might not be able to handle the discipline problems within a regular K-12 school, you would do well to consider adult education. Be aware, however, that in some ways it requires more patience than teaching in the regular school program. The students vary more in background and even in ability than in a regular high school program. This may be a plus or a minus to you as the teacher. These students may already have advanced degrees but may want to study for a particular license, learn to paint in watercolors or learn to use a computer. They are in school by their own free will, and on one hand, their intrinsic motivation does seem to make the classes easier to teach. On the other hand the large variety in the class can make it more difficult. Some of the students may feel that they know more, especially about life, than you do and try to take over the class. Some of the students may be older than you or better educated but you must always remember you have a special ability that they desire to learn.

The pay for both substitute teaching and the teaching of adult education classes is drastically lower than that for teaching in regular K-12 programs but such teaching will give you an opportunity to test your interests and develop your ability. Teaching is one area where, except for vocational programs, little credit is given to you for work out of the field. There will most probably be no benefits such as medical insurance unless you have a full-time licensed position. Your salary level will usually not depend on your years of experience but you will be placed on a pay level based on your teaching experience at a flat rate which is set by the school board.

Unless there is a general increase, there will be no raises from term to term-based on your outstanding performance.

Some second career areas really relate to old dreams. A friend of mine (I'll tell you that she has a son thirty years old just to give you an idea of her age) has just developed a night club act with another woman. Both of these women have other lives and jobs, but they have put together a comedy act and are doing performances on the weekends at condominiums and local women's groups. They are planning to do their routine on a cruise ship in the near future. They wish they had been doing this all of their lives. They will never get rich performing on the condominium circuit, but it has brought a great deal of satisfaction and excitement into their lives and pleasure into the lives of their audience.

A young man I know who works in a restaurant three nights a week is a dancer and a choreographer during the day. He hopes that someday he will be able to make a living in his profession of dancing. He is not involved in a career change but he has to make do with a job he considers tedious until he can exist on the income from the career he really desires and in which he engages part-time.

119

The ministry seems to be an area a number of people are entering as a second career. I know several people who have gone into the ministry after successful careers in other areas. Some of these people were not able to enter the ministry on a full-time basis when they first started out in the ministry. They obtained their training and began serving on a part-time basis in small churches, being a substitute minister for someone on vacation or ill or during part of the year in a tourist area.

Some of these part-time ministers have unusual backgrounds. One extremely successful minister, with an extensive parish and television ministry, was a dance teacher before he decided to change his career. Many remember the beginnings of the little parish he started, which has grown so extraordinarily over the years, and now includes a large television ministry as part of his church.

Another friend who used to sell real estate has started a new business making and creating unique stuffed sculptures including bears and lions. Her talents have led her to national prominence in this area and she gives presentations all over the country relating to her unusual techniques for making these wonderful creatures.

Following Your Dreams, Part-time

Everyone has dreams, but not everyone is able to follow them on a full-time basis. Some people are moving into the second career because they were not able to follow their original dreams years ago. Others are only discovering their new careers now.

The creative arts are the most difficult to pursue as a new career. There are two reasons for this. Not only is it intrinsically more difficult to switch to this area later in life but also it is not fun to starve in an attic when you are making a switch.

Arts and Crafts as a Part-time Career

If you are involved in an art or a craft, you may find yourself working on a part-time basis. You can make your items during the week, in the evenings perhaps, and sell them at various arts and crafts fairs on the weekend. Many people enjoy selling at the fairs and you will soon build up a following. I always remember an artist I knew who was a postal worker but enjoyed painting. As a lark, he took some of his work to a local show one weekend and sold the pieces for far more than he had earned that week. He began to paint more pictures using a particular style which seemed to be attractive to his customers. He continued to sell more and gradually began to go to shows farther from his home. He also was able to raise the price of his work. Eventually he quit his regular job and spent his full time painting and selling. He always remembered the first time he came back home to his family after a show. He brought his wife into the bedroom and began to pull out money from various pockets and from his shoes where he had hidden it, afraid of being robbed. His wife was amazed. She couldn't believe that he could have made so much. Soon she was going with him, having quit her minimum wage job. She turned out to have much more talent than he had at selling his paintings and keeping the records. He continued to paint at the shows, but he had to be careful not to reveal the secrets of his special technique. Together they were a great team. They paid someone to take care of their children on the weekends. Now she could be home with her children all week and they had a much better lifestyle. It was a wonderful time for them. It meant taking a chance when he gave up his job in the post office with its great benefits, but they didn't do it full time until they were certain they could make a better living without the regular job. I have lost track of them, but I hope their success is continuing.

Some people do not like to try and sell their own products. It is possible for them to sell through specialty shops and through direct orders placed in response to advertisements in crafts magazines. There are a number of books which list sources for arts and craft sales. The magazines in a particular specialty are a good source of the names of outlets for these products.

The internet has opened up vast possibilities for artists and crafters. People have often started small internet businesses in their spare time with little investment and have seen these businesses grow. They are not giants like Microsoft, but they are stable little businesses. It all means hard work but it is satisfying. A more complete discussion of internet businesses will be found in another chapter.

Free-lance Writing as a Part-time Career

Although professional artists are somewhat deprecating of the "Sunday painter," the same does not apply to writers. Very few writers are able to pursue that art as a full-time career. Writing is an area which gives great satisfaction, but does not provide a living wage to most of its practitioners. For some people, the pride of seeing something they have written is (almost) enough.

Writing lends itself to being both a second career and a sideline. It appears that it does not take much preparation to write. You can jot down the exact phrase you need for the opening sentence of your work on the back of a napkin at lunch or on the flap of an old envelope. This of course is not true. Writers constantly take courses to develop their craft and to learn to prepare material that will be chosen by editors, but writers do not need to have a formal degree in writing. Much of writing is thinking...and rewriting. Don't be afraid that someone will laugh at you if you begin to write. Writing can bring you great satisfaction of itself. Getting something published is a wonderful feeling. Begin by joining writers groups or taking classes given by professional writers. Find a class that suits your needs and listen to what you are told, but do not give up your own individuality and creativity. You may not make it in a national magazine with your first published piece or have your first book hit the Best Seller list, but that is no reason for you to stop writing. Along with the pleasure of writing itself, you meet many enjoyable people.

Other Sidelines

Don't think that only the arts will yield a good sideline for you. You might consider a field such as automobile mechanics, computer repair, software development, tutoring or catering. Remember catering is how Martha Stewart started and look what a profitable career that has resulted in for her.

Exercise 10.1

Write down ten "sidelines" which you might be interested in pursuing. These may be old dreams or areas in which you have talent or knowledge. Remember, I am not suggesting that you pursue more than one area but I want you to consider several options before choosing one.

1._____
2._____
3._____
4._____
5._____
6. _____
7._____

8._____

9._____

10._____

Exercise 10.2

Put the sidelines in order according to the ones in which you have the most talent.

1._____

2._____

3._____

4._____

5._____

6._____

7._____

8._____

9._____

10._____

123

Exercise 10.3

Put the areas in order as to which ones you anticipate to be the most enjoyable for you.

1._____

2._____

3._____

4._____

5._____

6._____

7._____

8._____

9._____

10._____

Exercise 10.4

What would you have to do to be able to pursue each of theses areas? This might include taking classes, getting licensed, traveling to shows on weekends, renting space, etc.

1._____
2._____
3._____
4._____
5._____
6._____
7._____
8._____
9._____
10._____

124

Exercise 10.5

Reviewing the lists you have made, select one or two sidelines you would like to pursue.

Part-time Career vs. Hobby

The Internal Revenue Service has some specific guidelines on hobby and craft sidelines which you should review. You can get a pamphlet from the IRS regarding this matter. Learn what receipts you must save and what taxes you must pay, Can you deduct car expenses for travelling to craft shows to sell or workshop expenses or expenses for the use of your home. If you run your sideline as a business according to their rules, they will be happy. It you use the sideline as a source of tax deduc-

tions only and do not ever generate income from them, the IRS becomes generally unhappy and does not allow the deductions. They do, however, give you a reasonable time to achieve some success. Even the IRS realizes that working with sidelines does not bring instant income.

Another benefit to beginning a second career as a sideline is that you develop a record of experience in the new career area. You will now have something to fill in on your resume in that field. The experience may help you make up some of the lost time in the new area and begin at more than the entry level salary.

If you are trying to decide whether or not to pursue a second career and have some reservations about giving up your present position, think of a way you could do it on a part-time basis. Beginning your second career as a sideline may give you confidence in your ability to perform in the new career area and show you whether or not you really will find that career satisfactory.

Besides income, there are many benefits to entering the new career field slowly through a second job or sideline. It certainly is not possible in every field, but it occurs more often than you might expect.

Chapter 11
Starting Your Own Business

For many, the selection of a new career is linked to the desire to become their own boss, to own their own business, or to have a high ranking position in a company. To accomplish this, they either start their own business or buy a small business. Those who become writers or artists or produce a craft, also experience these desires to some degree. To accomplish this, they generally start their own business. Since their product is based on their own talent, they usually do not buy a business unless it is a gallery. These people experience the same problems associated with small businesses as the person who decides to open a hardware store or a garage. This subject is extremely complex and will only be discussed briefly in this book. If you are considering opening a business as your new career, I recommend that you read some of the books that have been published on the matter. The government has several booklets on small businesses and many colleges and adult education programs offer non-credit and credit courses in running your own small business. Groups, such as those composed of retired executives, offer help to individuals who are just starting their businesses or who are having difficulty in making necessary decisions.

Many of the taxing agencies offer courses covering the federal, state and local taxes you will have to pay and the forms you will have to submit on time. The last two words "on time" are very important. There are many forms which you have to fill out and they all have to be submitted on time or there will be very large penalties. Since money is always scarce when a person is starting a new business, you certainly don't want to throw it away on interest and penalties. Licenses are another issue. Even if you do not need a professional license to operate. you will certainly need occupational licenses (city and county) and the place you select for your business location must meet the zoning laws for your community and you may have to have sufficient parking. It is possible in some communities to run your business from your home but there are very specific rules. In my community, I can run my law practice from my home but I cannot have employees nor can I have clients come to my house. I meet them in other locations, such as in their offices, in a conference room which I rent from another attorney just for the purpose of the meeting, or meet them for lunch at which time we discuss their problem. Most of my clients have been with me for many and we do all of our discussions by telephone and fax. If you choose to have an internet based business or a mail-order business or a business which you run at art and craft shows, you may not need a business location.

128

Small businesses are the fastest growing component of the American business community. Unfortunately they are also the fastest failing component of the same community.

There are many good reasons for starting your own business. You may be out of work and believe that having your own business will bring some badly needed income to you. You may be planning for your retirement years and want to give the business to your children or sell it to generate a retirement income. You may see a unique opportunity to offer a service or product that is needed and not being provided in your community.

There are certain characteristics of a successful small business operator which are important, such as the ability to make decisions as needed, that is, instantly, to organize, to take risks, to seek rewards, to roll with the punches, to have great attention to details, to accept responsibility, and to show perseverance. Perhaps most important of all, is the characteristic of humility. You may believe that your mousetrap is the most wonderful one ever made but you have to be realistic about your abil-

ity to sell it. Enthusiasm is another important characteristic. When you are painting and decorating your new store, you will certainly be enthusiastic but when you
have taken in $7.95 as your day's total profit, your mood is certain to change. If you
are subject to moods of depression, running your own business may not be the career
for you. Some of the weaknesses that lead to failure in your own small business are:

- Working without a good business plan or even knowing what one is
- Tolerating too many interruptions or diversions
- Having unrealistic time frames for success
- Not having enough money to begin the business
- Not having enough money to carry on the business for at least a year without showing
  a profit
- Not having enough money or other resources to cover your own salary for at least a year
- Not being organized
- Not being able to deal with customers or employees
- Not being able to make good instant decisions
- Not admitting when you need to change a decision
- Not doing enough research on your product or service and the need of the community
  for that product or service
- Not correctly analyzing the location of your business (this is really worth a whole chapter
  of its own)
- Not following through
- Not being able to plan ahead

Running your own business demands a great deal of time and of energy. Go
down the list and check off your strengths and weaknesses. Where do you fit?

Be honest with yourself. Why are you really starting this business? If it is to cut
back on the number of hours you are working, cancel any idea you may have of going
into business. First of all it will be a 24/7 job, that is a twenty-four hours a day, seven
day a week commitment. If you are an artist and you think it will give you time to
paint, don't plan on it for having time to paint will mean you don't have customers.
If you are going to open a bookstore because you love to read or are a budding author,
don't plan on being able to doing these things and run a successful business.

If you are going to buy a business, make a very careful analysis of why that business is being sold. Also go over the books of the business very carefully. You will have an accountant but if you can't understand these books (and later your own books) you will have little chance of success. If numbers are your downfall take a simple accounting course before starting your business so that you will have at least some rudimentary knowledge of business procedures.

The seller of a business you are considering to buy may tell you that it is a cash business and that it makes a great deal more money than the books reflect. Don't believe him. It will be very nice for you if this is true (and don't forget every state gets very upset if the laws regarding sales tax are not followed and the IRS wants correct income reported) but don't believe it. The business must stand on the books as presented. Be very particular about the location. Is the business being sold because the owner has gotten so rich he or she is going to retire to an island they have bought or has the struggle to make the business successful finally become too much for the owner? Why do you think you can make it a success when others have failed in the same business at the same location? If you are buying a restaurant, for example, why do you think people will forget how bad the food and service was and come try out your spectacular improvements? Was it the location or the parking that kept the business from being successful? That is something you cannot overcome with your friendly nature. The same consideration goes for whatever type of business you are considering buying. Starting a business is not so hard, keeping that business running and lucrative is very difficult.

Finding the Time

Time, the monster that controls our lives, will be of particular importance when you start a new business. Suddenly you will not only be the boss, but you may be the only employee.

You may find yourself doing many tasks, and some of them may be the very ones you are seeking to escape. The boss in a new company rarely works decent hours. Being a boss is not a nine to five job. If you don't do the task yourself, you will have to pay someone to do it, and that brings us to the second point for discussion.

Finding the Money

Money is always a serious topic today. The cost of borrowing money has caused changes in the way many companies, even large corporations and governments, do business. Some very large concerns, for example, no longer accept credit cards. Don't forget it costs you money to accept credit cards but few businesses could survive without them. Check with a business oriented bank which handles credit count accounts for small businesses to determine the costs. Remember that a customer can try to cancel the charge even a couple of months after the sale if they are able to say there was something wrong with the product. If you are going to start a business you will need to have sufficient capital available, in spite of the high cost of borrowing. Insufficient capital or an inability to maintain inventory has caused businesses to fold. These businesses would have been successful if they could have weathered various crises by having sufficient capital. You will have to produce a business plan. There are computer software programs that will help you form this plan but you need to have a good understanding of a business plan, either through your own reading or through taking a course, before you can use the software to your advantage. The process of producing the business plan will help you understand the complexities of your proposed business and the things you must plan for.

131

Finding the Right Location

If you are going to open a store that will either be based on your own talents and products or those of others, you will have to pay close attention to location. People are conscious of both safety and travel time these days, and no one will beat a path to anybody's door any more no matter how good the mousetrap. They might be able to buy as good a product on the Internet but that is part of another chapter. A good location will undoubtedly be expensive, but it may be a necessity for success. You may, however, decide that you do not want to pay a great deal of rent. You may have to realize that in order to build the business, you will not be taking much money home for yourself for a long time, perhaps as long as a year. You will probably need two to two and a half times the money you originally estimated that you will need to start the business.

The best location may turn out to be a virtual one. Many new businesses are starting on the Internet. Some of these are successful and others fail just as with a business that is located in a specific location but at least you don't have to worry about getting mugged in your business's parking lot or being stuck with a long term lease. The next chapter will discuss starting a business on the internet.

Federal and state tax laws will demand a great deal of attention on your part. There are requirements for workman's compensation, unemployment, and health insurance policies, and other benefits which you will have to follow. You will either have to keep your own books and tax records or hire an accountant to do it. The number of forms you have to submit seems to increase yearly. Not filing the correct form at the right time can bring about penalties and use up money that you can ill-afford to give away.

Working with Family Members

If you are going to work in a business with other members of your family, be certain you can work together on this intimate a basis. Such endeavors have brought trouble to formerly peaceful families. Family businesses have been the backbone of this country, but you should be aware of anticipated difficulties and try to solve problems before they start. Being the boss may result in family strife, especially if the family members are the employees.

Although I may sound negative, I don't mean to be. I have seen a number of people try to start businesses without sufficient capital and without realizing how much time it would take from their lives. I wish to caution you to watch for the pitfalls. Having your own business can be the most satisfying experience, and it can also bring you great fortune that cannot be matched by salary. It can bring you considerable pride and satisfaction and it may be work that you like. You can always make yourself president. It can be a great experience, but it also can be a disaster.

Hiring People to Work for You

As a small business owner you will have to hire people. Don't be too quick to hire. Study the requirements of the job you need done and be certain to get a person who can fill all those requirements for you.

Be certain that you do some cash flow planning. You may, at the end of the year, 133 have made enough money to pay all of the bills but if you haven't had the money in hand on time, you will have a serious cash flow problem and may lose sources of your materials or inventory. You may also get sued and may eventually go bankrupt. You have to pay your employees on a timely basis as agreed to, like every week or every month and you have to make the tax payments on the salary you pay yourself and others. Delaying making these deposits can be disastrous. There is also a matter of paying sales tax on your sales or services at the required time. There may even be criminal penalties if you do not make these payments at the time required. Good records must be kept in these areas and calculations made on the back of an envelope won't do. Cash flow is a serious matter. Not having the money when it is needed to pay salaries, taxes, and for inventory can force you to close your business. Having future payments coming in may not be enough to save your business if the money arrives to late.

Cost and operation control is also a very important matter to learn. Don't learn it when you are in financial problems. Do it right from the beginning.

To Incorporate or Not to Incorporate

Whether or not to incorporate your business is a question which overwhelms many people. "I'm not General Motors" they say. "Why would I need to incorporate?" "It is too complicated." "It is too expensive."

The only disadvantage I can think of with regard to incorporating is the cost and that can be minimal. If you do not incorporate your business, it will be called a sole proprietorship. Linked to you personally, it may create liability for you.

Incorporating a business will not protect you from lawsuits regarding personal negligence, such as your using a truck in your business which has bald tires and brakes which you know are faulty or from contracts which you signed personally as well as on behalf of the corporation, but it will protect yourself and your assets from many other types of lawsuits. If you have more than one business, you must not mix your assets and this will be much easier to accomplish if each business is incorporated. If you want to expand your business, it may be easier to get a loan if the business is incorporated. When you come to sell your business, it will be much easier to sell either the stock in the corporation or the assets of the corporation rather than to sell a sole proprietorship. If you do not incorporate, you will still have the costs of selecting a "fictitious name" which must be advertised and registered with the state. If you use a fictitious name and build the reputation of your company, you will still run the risk of someone else incorporating that name in your state. Even if you are the first to use it, in most states, they will have the right to incorporate under that name if you have not incorporated.

You may incorporate a business in the state in which you live, the state in which you are going to operate the business, and any other state you choose. There are some complicated tax advantages to incorporating in such states as Delaware and Arizona but if you are starting a small business, these advantages most probably won't apply to you and I'm not certain that they apply to most businesses any more.

134

Few attorneys and accountants who handle incorporations can explain the advantages. If you incorporate in a state other than the state in which you are going to operate your business you will still have to register with the state in which you are going to do business as a "foreign corporation." Being a "foreign corporation" does not mean that your business is incorporated or set up in some foreign country but only that it has been set up in another state. There are a number of books which show you how to incorporate and the state statute is often very clear about what must be in the incorporation papers so that you can create the incorporation document yourself and file it your self. There are also examples that can be found in books on starting a business which you can follow. The filing fee will be different in each state but it is not astronomical and usually ranges from less than a hundred dollars to three or four hundred in most states. Even if you are having an attorney or an accountant perform this for you, check for the fees with the secretary of state's office for your state. In addition, you will get a bill for renewal each year that also is not very large. Arrange to have it sent to you instead of to your attorney or accountant and you won't be charged by them for paying a bill for you. Each state will have a different minimal number of directors that it requires in order to incorporate. In Florida, for example, this number is one. Their names and addresses will have to be listed in the incorporation papers along with the name of an incorporator, which may be yourself or the attorney or accountant who is handling the matter, and the name of a registered agent who must live in the state and who will accept service of process on behalf of the corporation. if you are registering in a state other than the one in which you live you will usually have to retain someone to act as registered agent. there are companies which do this for a small fee.

There are tax issues which must be decided such as whether you want to be a "c-corporation" or an "s-corporation." Being an "s-corp" can be very beneficial for a small business but it is not always the right decision. Eligibility to be an "s corp" is determined by Internal Revenue regulations and has nothing to do with state law. This issue is one that should be determined between you and your lawyer or tax accountant

135

unless you can get good information about the matter and make that decision by yourself.

If you are seriously considering starting your own business, plan those aspects we have discussed–the time, the money, the location, the regulations, and the opportunities. Can you do it all? It may be years before your business shows a profit. That is not a mark of failure, but is common for new businesses. Can you exist without any real income for a year or two while you are simultaneously putting money into the company? These are important questions, ones which you must answer before you take the final steps and establish yourself as boss.

Remember that the man or woman who works for him or herself has a difficult boss. Attend workshops in many areas on concerns like keeping tax records or formulating a business plan. You don't have to get a college degree in business first. If you are considering starting your own business or buying someone else's, it is essential that you attend some of the workshops in a variety of the areas that you must understand to operate your business. These workshops will help you to understand just what you are getting into. The small business administration which provides loans to small business owners conducts many useful workshops which you may be able to attend as well as those offered for free by community colleges and universities.

Each year thousands of businesses open, and each year thousands close. They are not necessarily the same businesses, of course. In today's economy it is very difficult to successfully start a business. If this is your choice for a second career, go cautiously and be aware of all the demands it will make on you personally and financially. Even if you know how to sell your product or service very well you will have a great many specialized areas to study. You will have to become an accountant, a psychologist, a decorator, carpenter, painter, a marketing expert, a financial expert, a trainer, a personnel manager, and a person who can put in a day's work after staying up half the night doing records and tax reports.

Chapter 12

Starting an Internet Business

What Makes an Internet Business Special

*I*f you listen to the news at all these days, you will hear discussion of "dot com businesses." These are businesses that make use of the Internet to both advertise and sell their products or services. The name is taken from the most common form of internet addresses which is "name.com." While it appears that a dot com business requires very little startup money, that is often not true. In addition to the startup money the continuing costs of inventory and employees have caused many dot com businesses to fail this year. Their failure is specifically for the same reasons that non-internet businesses fail. If you are not trying to start another amazon.com or e-bay.com but are trying to start a small business, there is better hope for success although you may not be making enormous sums of money from it. Gradual growth is usually the best policy.

Planning for gradual growth permits the person starting an internet business to begin with a modest amount of money and time involved. For many, the internet business begins as a "sideline, " that is, as a second job perhaps in an area of special interest.

Many women who want to stay at home with young children find an Internet business meets their needs. While the person may be working at home, it is certain that children do not stay quiet and organized most of the time. It may be difficult to give the business the concentration it needs if children are simultaneously demanding attention. For those who have children in school for part of the day, it will be ideal, permitting the parent to work on the internet business and product during the school hours while simultaneously allowing the parent to be home when the children are home.

It is also ideal for the person seeking a second job. That person is home and working on the second job and can allot the time to personal pursuits and the second job as he or she desires. Although the business may start slowly, it is possible that it will soon do well enough that it becomes the primary job.

The internet business may bring special satisfaction to the person starting it. While they may not be interested in leasing a store and sitting there all day, the Internet will give them both privacy and publicity. If they are involved in arts and crafts, they will have a much larger client base for their work than if they rented a location and even if they showed their work at fairs. Weekend exposure at fairs and having an Internet business often provides the ideal combination for arts and crafts based businesses.

It is also possible to expand an existing business by using the Internet. I have a friend who has owned a second hand bookstore for many years. Customers would often ask her to find a particular book for them, perhaps to complete a series or because they liked the author. When she became computer and Internet literate, she began to use the Internet to find books on the Internet for her customers for a small charge. She then got her own Homepage and she started getting customers from all over the world who did not have a source for these books in their own area. Her business has expanded so that she now ships books all over the world on a regular basis. Although she has considered closing her store and just dealing on the Internet, her store has also grown and she has had to remodel so as to have more display area. Customers who know her business from the Internet, make it a point to visit her retail store when they are in the geographic area, resulting in the growth of both aspects of her business. Her store has become much better known locally without any expensive advertising on her part.

Another friend, Malacky Kearns, who made the bodhrans and other drums for the original Irish and American productions of Riverdance, lives in a beautiful but isolated little village on the west coast of Ireland. He does not have much hope of "walk in" traffic and occasionally used to appear at a show or festival to present his bodhrans to the public. That is how I first met him. This has become unnecessary since he started his homepage and people from all over the world have become aware of his work. He is linked to many other Irish sites. Stores, especially in the more heavily tourist areas, now carry many of his musical instruments whereas formerly they only had a few for sale because now customers come in asking for his work. As for the "walk-ins", many people go out of their way to visit the village of Roundtree to see how the borans are made and to purchase a signed one from the man himself.

Not everyone may be as successful as these two friends of mine but the potential is there. Each of these people used the Internet to expand an existing business. They already had the knowledge they needed to run their business and acquired the necessary computer knowledge so that they could expand their world class exposure by using the Internet.

A person starting a business on the Internet must learn all of the standard aspects of their business as well as the computer based aspects.

Advantages and Disadvantages of an internet business

Businesses which operate on the internet only, have all of the same considerations and concerns as those which have a physical location for their operations. All of the topics discussed in the chapter on starting your own business apply with some additional "twists."

As a business owner, you may consider the factor of isolation which comes with an Internet business a plus or a minus. It is possible to dress casually while operating your business. Those commercials with people working in their night-clothes are quite realistic. Unless you want to provide a phone number, you may also be spared the incessant ringing of the telephone, usually with a person trying to sell you something on the other end of the line. As mentioned before, the business can be started with little capital and you can ration the time you spend according to how fast you want the business to grow. It also gives you an opportunity to experiment with your products, especially handmade items without having anyone insult your creativity.

There are, however, many things you must learn. Even selecting the address for your homepage requires some consideration and new knowledge.

When you choose a name for your business, you will also have to choose an internet name as well. Just as you will have to compete for a name for an incorporated business or a fictitious name, now you will have to add the extra chore of finding a unique internet address for your business as well. Your e-mail address is limited by your internet provider, but the address for your business's homepage will be far more limited. If you are using ".com" as the suffix, you must follow the rules of the company that provides the ".com" addresses. If you choose another company to provide this service, your name will have their rules to follow. The ".com" names have gone fast and you may find the name you want is already gone and so are all of the alternates you can think of. This doesn't mean that the name for your business must be different but that the address used so that your prospective clients can reach you must be unique. It should also give customers a good indication of what the business does.

If you want potential customers to find you, you have to get linked with other businesses and listed on a large variety of search engines. Getting all of these things listed is an enormous job but the success of your internet business will depend on it. This chapter is only meant to give you the briefest taste of what you will need to do.

The selection of computer hardware and software and the

design of your homepage also require special knowledge. It may be wise to hire a consultant to design your homepage and get it operational as well as having someone assist you in the selection of the computer and the software you will run on that machine. You may need all kinds of peripherals including a digital camera and scanner. Starting an Internet business may give you the excuse to purchase all of these devices but remember to review the IRS rules when you take your deductions.

This chapter is only meant to give you a taste of what running an Internet business can mean to you.

141

Chapter 13
Decision Helper

A Number Game

Now we are going to play a "number game" with the careers which remain on your lists. If you are absolutely terrified of doing any math, you do not have to do this exercise. You are the master of yourself in this book. Before you decide, read the section and follow the example. It is easier to do than you may think. If you are willing to try doing it, I believe you will find it fun. You may also find that the results are enlightening. I have taught this exercise to students many times over the years. The non-math types are always reluctant at first. They need encouragement. But many of them, after they learn how really easy it is, have later told me that they have used it for all kinds of decisions.

You do not need to follow the results of this game. The choice of a new career is too important for that, but the analysis you will have to do to get your numbers will reveal a number of things to you.

The results of this exercise will give you some insight into your true feelings. You may need a calculator to carry this out. It is a little program which I call "Decision Helper." As you read each step below peek at the example so that you can really understand it. You will find that it is easier than you think.

Decision Helper: going on a Vacation

In order to give you a little practice, we are going to use the decision helper with a task such as choosing a place to go on vacation. I have nine days for vacation and I live in Florida.

Think about four places I would like to visit: I picked New York City, St. Augustine, Washington, D.C., North Carolina Mountains. The characteristics I selected were cost, seeing new places, able to drive there, getting a rest, climate. I am twenty-eight years old and single. I will travel with a friend in August.

This is my chart in the beginning:

Table 13.1

Vacation: Decision Chart No.1

	Impt.	NYC.	St. A beach	W.D.C.	N.C. Mts.
Cost	10	4	7	5	9
New Places	8	7	5	7	4
able to Drive	9	4	8	5	8
Rest	5	3	9	3	8
Climate	7	5	8	4	9

I ranked cost as a 10 since I do not have much money. Because it may be cheaper for me to drive and I may need a car except in New York and Washington, I will rank that a 9, seeing new places is an 8, getting a rest is a 5, climate is a 7 (since I live in Florida I don't want it too be too hot. for my vacation.)

Washington in August is hot, nobody gets any rest in either New York or in Washington, D.C. and even if you have been there before, there are always new things to see.

Now multiply the weighing factor by the factor for each place and write in a second column under each place

144

Table 13.2

Vacation: Decision Chart No.2

		NYC.	St. ABeach	W.D.C.	N.C. Mts.
Cost	10	4 40	7 28	5 20	9 36
New Places	8	7 56	5 40	7 56	4 32
able to Drive	9	4 35	8 72	5 45	8 72
Rest	5	3 15	9 45	3 15	8 40
Climate	7	5 35	7 49	4 28	9 56
Totals		**181**	**234**	**164**	**236**

While the North Carolina Mountains came out first with a 236, St. Augustine Beach came out a quite close second and you might want to consider both. While getting rest was not so important, it was a strong point with both of these places but it was really cost that tipped the balance. New York and Washington are both expensive places to stay and you would have to fly there and not have a car available for getting around. While a car would be impossible to park except for high parking fees, getting around by cab or even public transportation would also be very expensive. You undoubtedly would have selected other places and other important characteristics but this example allows you to see how it is done.

Exercise 13.1

Work out a decision assist table for your choice of vacation. You can go anywhere and have any number of characteristics for your decision.

Decision Helper Choosing a career

Don't be afraid—an example will be given!

STEP I

Identify the careers which you are evaluating. Include your current career if you have one Write them down using a single word identifier that will bring the concept of the career clearly to your mind. You may include as many careers as you wish.

STEP 2

Identify the characteristics of the new career which would be important to you. Express these characteristics in one or two word phrases. Include all of the characteristics that are important to you. They might be such things as "salary", "free time", "creativity", etc.

STEP 3

On a scale of 1 to 10 choose a weighing factor for each of the characteristics. You may want to select the characteristic that is most important and give it a 10 or you may not. You can give the same weighing factor to more than one characteristic. For example two characteristics could be a 9. You can give decimal weighing factors to characteristics. For example, you could use a 7.5 as a weighing factor. It is subjective. How important is that characteristic to you compared to the other characteristics you have written down?

STEP 4

Now you need to take a large piece of paper and make some columns. You will need a column for the characteristics and a column for the weighing factors. You will need two columns for each of the careers. For the mathematically minded, if N is the number of careers you have you will need $2 \times N + 2$ columns. For example, if the number of careers you are evaluating is 7, you would need $2 \times 7 + 2 = 16$ columns. Make your chart large. Tape some pieces of paper together if necessary. It isn't of any use to you if you can't read it.

The number of rows you will need is calculated differently. You will need a row for the headings, a row for every characteristic and a row for the total. If C is the number of characteristics, then the total number of rows is $C + 2$. If $C = 6$, then you will need 8 rows.

Now put the headings over the columns. Over the first column put the word characteristics, over the second column put the words weighing factor, over the next two columns put the first career word, over the next two columns put the second career word, etc.

In the first column under the heading "characteristics", list the characteristics on each of the rows. In the very last row write "total." In the second column, under the heading "weighing factor", write in the weighing factor you selected for each characteristic. Now you are ready to begin evaluating the careers.

STEP 5

Consider the first career with respect to the first characteristic. In your judgment, how does it do on a scale from 1 to 10? Is it a really a "super" career or just so-so? Pick your number for that characteristic. This is the weighing factor for that characteristic. Write that number down on the first row in the first column under that career heading. For example, suppose the first characteristic you have written down is pay and suppose you gave that characteristic a weighing factor of 8. Suppose the first career you think about is computer programming. Ask yourself how computer programming rates with regard to pay. Perhaps you give it an 8.5. Put an 8.5 down in the first column under computer programming and in the row marked pay.

147

Now comes the step that has been known to confuse some people. If you don't understand exactly what I am doing, don't worry about it. Once you follow the steps in the example you will understand the process. Multiply the score for the career on a certain characteristic by the weighing factor for that same characteristic. This is the weighing factor written at the beginning of that row. Put your answer in the second column under that career heading. If the weighing factor was an 8 and the score was 8.5, then the number you will put in this column is 8 x 8.5 = 68.

Now go down to the next row and take a look at the second characteristic. Give the career a score on the second characteristic. Put the answer in the first column for the career and in the row headed by the characteristic. Multiply the score by the weighing factor for that characteristic. This is the weighing factor in that row and column. Put that answer in the second column under that career heading which is the third column on your paper.

Continue to fill in all the numbers for the characteristics for that career and then move to the other careers.

STEP 6

Under each career heading, add up the numbers in the second column under the career heading. These were the numbers that resulted when you multiplied the weighing factor by the score of each career on each characteristic. Put the totals in the row marked "totals" in second column under each career heading.

STEP 7

Compare your answers for the totals. Put the careers in order according to the totals. Do you agree with your results? Is the career that came out highest the one you think is the best for you? It would appear to be, but there is still a subjective element.

Decision Helper: An Example of Career Selection

Henry Jones has an associates degree from a community college. He is presently employed as a construction worker, but he is considering changing his job. He has identified that he is good at mathematics and is willing to go back to school in order to be prepared to enter a new career.

Henry has identified the following career areas as being interesting to him, including his present one: construction, electronic technology, computer programming, computer operator, purchasing, accounting, and automotive factory work. These become the headings for columns in the chart below.

The characteristics of the job that are important to him have been identified (in any order) as pay, geographic location, security, repetition of tasks, fringe benefits, more education, creating things, future advancement, pride. These are the headings for the rows. See the chart below.

The entries under weighing factor were decided by Henry on the basis of his feelings only, rather than any outside influences or standards. Pay and future are important. If a career demanded a great deal mor education, Henry saw that as a negative and gave it a small number. Someone else might have given it a large number.

Table 13.3

Decision Chart No.1 for Henry Jones

Value •	Construction •	Elec. Tech. •	Computer Operator •	Purchasing •	Accounting
Pay	8				
Location	5				
Security	8				
Repetition	4				
Fringe Ben.	6				
Education	6				
Creating	3				
Advancement	7				
Pride	6.5				

If Henry now begins the next step (Step 5), he will have to decide how construction ranks on each of the characteristics. You can see how he ranked things in Table 10.2.

Table 13.4

Decision Chart No.2 for Henry Jones

Characteristic	Value •	Construction •	Elec. Tech. •	Computer Operator •	Purchasing •	Accounting
Pay.	8	8				
Location	5	6				
Security	8	8				
Repetition	4	4				
Fringe Benefits	6	3				
Education	6	10				
Creating	3	5				
Advancement	7	1				
Pride	6.5	4				
Totals						

Note that since no education was necessary for Henry, a "10" was given for that characteristic under construction.

In order to obtain the value for the second column under the first career, you have to multiply the value in the first column under the career by the weighing factor for that row. You can then add the second column to get a total value for Henry's choices.

Table 13.5

Decision Chart No.3 for Henry Jones

Characteristic	Value	Construction	Elec. Tech.	Computer Operator	Purchasing	Accounting
Pay	8	8	64			
Location	5	6	30			
Security	8	8	64			
Repetition	4	4	16			
Fringe Benefits	6	3	18			
Education	6	10	60			
Creating	3	5	15			
Advancement	7	1	7			
Pride	6.5	4	26			
Total			300			

150

The total for construction would be 300. Remember that the values of these numbers are entirely Henry's. Someone else may have had a higher or a lower value for each of the items. Henry would then complete his chart and put the careers in numerical order according to the totals.

Try this exercise with a number of careers at first, until you get used to the process. By the way, this technique can be used with a number of decisions you have to make. Try it with choosing a place for dinner, for example, but if you find it terribly confusing or if math is a large problem for you, skip this exercise. It is a useful exercise however and if you can get a friend to help you, do it. Once you get it under your control, you may use it for different decisions.

This process is really a simplified version of a more complicated decision program and is not fail-safe. It has some flaws but the alternative requires some very high-powered mathematics and probably the use of a computer and an ability to program. This process is fairly straightforward and serves to give you another instrument, a very subjective instrument, to use in your selection of a career.

Try this with your own career choices. How does it come out? Do you object to the result? If so, then you have some conscious or unconscious bias toward the items on your list. It is good to have such feelings. At the least, the calculations will cause you to react negatively toward some items on your list and positively toward others. It will help you select from your list. And, yes, it will help you to make a shorter list.

The "Decision Helper" calculations will give you yet another list, one that ranks careers in order of their performance in the "Decision Helper" calculation described above. Use this list to further refine your choices.

Chapter 14
Change is a Family Affair

Considering Your Responsibilities

For many people the key to the selection of a career and the successful pursuit of that goal lies with the family unit. Family support can help make a dream come true while family opposition can attempt to destroy the dream. The young person making his or her first career choice is generally influenced by parents, older siblings, possibly other family members, friends, and teachers. There may be some person in his or her life who acts as a role model. Unless the young person is married, he or she is generally independent of a family unit. The degree of family responsibility for young people who are still single (or don't have a significant other)is usually minimal.

On the other hand, the person who makes a mid-life career change often has tremendous responsibilities with a wife or husband and children to consider. These people must also be consulted. His or her range of responsibilities is more extensive than the recent graduate. They have more to lose but in fact, they also have more to gain. The older person who is single and who is responsible for himself may be more burdened by stress than the younger career seeker. They may already be somewhat disillusioned because they are not satisfied with some aspects of their present life.

This person will have to continue to "make a living" for himself and it may be more difficult for him to change without the support of a family.

One may be legally free, think of one's self as liberated, an individual, but life and happiness still depends to a great extent on one's family. A career change often follows a divorce, although I have known instances where a divorce follows the career change.

When to Include Your Family

You may have noticed that I did not include the family in the very first steps of your career planning, which were described in the previous chapters. You may be able to involve some family members from the very first, but most people have to do much of the self-exploration on their own. They need to formulate a tentative plan before exposing their ideas and themselves to the opinions of their family.

154

We have discussed how ridicule can destroy dreams. Dreams are fragile. They must have some shape and form before you can reveal them. You must first establish confidence in your dream before you discuss it with a great number of people or you may be too easily dissuaded.

There are some questions which you must answer to your own satisfaction before you reveal your plans.

1. Who are the people in your family whose opinions are most important to you?
2. Whose are least important to you?
3. Who are the people in your family who will be most strongly affected by your change in career?
4. Who will react most strongly, either positively or negatively, to your announcement?
5. Who will be destructive?
6. Who will be supportive?

There may be very little overlap in your three lists, but there will be some people on each list who will have an important effect on your decision. For example, the change may affect your children greatly, but if they are very young, you would not be affected by their opinion. If they are older, they might have a great deal to contribute to your decision. You may have a brother-in-law who is negative about everything you do but he would not affect you directly because you don't like him. He might influence someone who would affect you, however, such as your husband or wife. A coach studies the opposing team very carefully. I do not mean to imply that members of your family are your opponents but you must be concerned with regard to the dynamics of the interaction. Remember the stress chart that was discussed previously. You need to minimize the stress in your life if you are going to make this change a successful one. You need to list the major individuals with whom you will have to interact on this matter. Which of them will influence your decision? To whom are you simply making the announcement without asking for any reaction. It is not reasonable to think you can avoid getting a reaction from most people–whether you want it or not, you will get it.

Think about these individuals carefully. What kind of a reaction do you think they will have with regard to this change you are planning? You are part of your family and your family is part of you. For some of you there may be tension already present in the family unit, which might be a source of some of your desire for change or uncertainty as to the selection of a career. Changing to a new career will temporarily add to the stress in the family unit although ultimately it may relieve some of the problems that are the source of the stress.

What made you begin to think about changing your career or selecting a career. Was the original desire to select or change your career your own idea? It may have been initiated by another person such as your wife or husband or your parents who are contributing towards the cost of your education. It may be someone else who feels that the change is necessary for you. There may be a desire for more income, less absence from home, a better future, more stability or more pride in your career. These desires may be expressed openly or they may be presented very subtlety. Given the dynamics of American society, this situation is true more often for men than for women.

Women are more likely to be personally unhappy with their present career or lack of career than men and come to the conclusion that they must change rather than to be pushed into change by another. Even if you feel that you are being given a slight shove in this direction, the decision to change may indeed be the correct one. Sometimes others know what is good for us before we ourselves ascertain it.

Be clear in your own mind about your family's feelings before you present your ideas to them. Everyone in your family is an individual, just as you are. Don't think of the others in your family or your close associates as "them". Think of each one as a person whose help you will need to make the choice and to make the transition. Those whom you know will never help you at least can usually be persuaded to make little trouble if it is handled correctly.

Your family is important to you and you are important to them. Any change you make in your life will affect your family and they may be frightened by the idea of change. They may feel insecure. They may not understand your level of unrest or boredom with your present position. Inadequate salary or opportunity for advancement are easy to explain but many sources of dissatisfaction with a position have much more subtle causes. These are often difficult to explain even to people who care about you. They are also difficult for someone who does not actually do your daily work tasks to understand. Try to work out some ways of explaining to them just why you are reluctant to stay with your present work or career and need to move to the new one.

156

A woman who desires a career may have a difficult time explaining her dissatisfaction with her present life to her husband. She may want to expand herself and gain more respect from the community through her new career. Her husband may believe that this desire reflects some inadequacy on his part or some ingratitude on hers. These feelings must be understood, but ultimately the person changing his or her career or selecting a career must decide what is best. Understand the motives behind some of the reactions you will get. Be firm in your reliance on your instincts.

Listen to Your Family's Reaction

The decision to change your lifestyle and select a career will ultimately be yours but do give serious attention to what your family and friends tell you. It is possible that they are more correct than you are willing to admit with respect to your choice of career. While they may have other motives, which they don't even realize, they may also be correct in what they are saying. Try to give an unbiased review of their ideas. They may know you at least as well as you know yourself. Understanding is the key word in getting your family to be on your side. Remember that your family may have delayed reaction to the suggested change. It may take a while for their reactions to really develop, either in a positive or in a negative manner.

At first some family members will at least be neutral if they are not positive to your ideas. As the change begins to take place, the family members may become concerned and express dissatisfaction with the concept of changing careers. This reaction may have its source in fear and that fear itself may have many sources.

Family members may fear you will fail in the career you have selected and that certain aspects of their own lives, such as income, will be worse than they were before. Another fear is that you will succeed in the career and that this success will leave no room in your life for that person. He or she may feel that you will not need that person as much in the future as you do now. This is a common fear of husbands whose wives enter an exciting career which makes them independent. Another emotion related to the career change of a family member is jealousy. Family members may be jealous not only of your success, but even of your ability to change some part of your life. They may not want to deprive you of this change but simply desire it for themselves. They may be in as much need of change as you are. The fact that they are not able to improve their own situation may have been accentuated by your change.

Others will worry that you will have less interest in them because of your interest in your new career. You may have less time to spend with them. You may have less money to spend on recreational activities. These may indeed be facts– not illusions. You will have to be sensitive to all possible reactions. Some of them may surprise you.

Do not forget that a negative reaction on the part of someone may be the right reaction. It is possible that the career you have chosen is not the right one for you.

157

It might be right for you and not right for your family. It might not be right for you. You will have to analyze your career choice in these terms.

I'm not sure how Gauguin's lifestyle change could be assessed. It probably was good for him, but not good for his family. No one interviewed him about that later in life, I suppose. He just left his family behind. Where did they get the financial support to live? Were they better off without him?

Any change will certainly be easier if you have your family on your side. You will have a better idea about your reasons for change if you involve your family in the decision-making process, and if you plan this change taking their feelings and needs into account.

Preparing for the Change

If your career change is going to require preparation such as returning to school, the situation will be further intensified. You will be taking time and money away from the family unit in order to prepare for your change and may encounter resistance. You may find it difficult to get the privacy to do the studying or preparation that you need for the new career. Some of the tasks that you have been doing may have to be taken over by others and there will be understandable resistance to this. The expenditure of both time and money will have to be planned for carefully.

Time, unlike money, is a difficult quantity to borrow. Your family needs you. If you have children they will only be young once. If you borrow too much time from the family unit it will have a negative effect on everyone's life. It is important to be aware of this and to make accommodations for it in your time plan.

The question of time-management and planning will be addressed elsewhere in this book but it has a substantial impact on your family's response.

Don't be surprised by negative reactions on the part of family members and friends or even by the butcher, the dentist or your favorite bartender. Everybody believes that they are entitled to an opinion and they will certainly be willing to share it with you.

Don't feel that your family does not love you if they are resistant either as indi-

158

viduals or as a family unit. They have their problems too. Be sensitive to them. Their love for you may be the very source of their negative reaction.

Before you present your plan, your dream, to even your closest loved one, be certain of what you really want to get from this change. You must be able to express clearly your reasons for your career selection. You must be able to describe what is wrong with your present job or career path. You must also have a good understanding of the new career or careers you are considering.

You should never give your family the impression that you made up your mind without talking to them, even if that is the case. That seems like a deceptive thing to say, but even if you are convinced you are making the right choice, you must give your family the opportunity to give you their ideas.

Unless you are used to family gatherings, it is better not to present your ideas in a group format.

You may want to begin by talking with someone in your family unit who will be supportive. You are looking for creative ideas for your own future. Even after reading the 20,000 entries in the *Dictionary of Occupational Titles*. you may still have passed over or not yet come across the position that is just right for you.

Evaluating Your Family's Reaction

Evaluate the situation. What is it that each member of your family will be most concerned with. Some may be jealous or fear your success. Some may fear you will not have time for them. Some may fear you will move away or leave them. This is a fear which will occur with both those who will move with you and those who will stay behind. Some may fear that there will be less money or that their life will change substantially. Evaluate these potential charges. Is there any truth in them? Are there ways in which you can minimize the negative effects of the change on others?

For some, this will be a very important consideration since they are anxious to sustain their family unit. Others may not even make this gesture since they consciously or unconsciously desire the separation of the family situation.

If there is already trouble in the family, this element of change may be sufficient to cause the final break. Be aware of this. For those who are not married, the break may be with parents or the "significant other." Again the question, what do you really want from this change? Is the career change important or is it a tool to effect a more substantial change in your life? This may be a good change. There are many single people who are unhappy who still live at home and who work in a family business. They might become happier people if they could find the career they really wanted all along and pursue it. A new career could mean a whole new life for them.

Friends can be just as much of a help or a hindrance as family. If you have close friends, they may be part of your extended family in influence if not in responsibility. Be cautious of negative comments from your friends. They may have your best interest at heart. They may be right. They may also be jealous without either you or they recognizing it. If the new career may seem to give you greater importance or financial reward, they may have subconscious feelings against it. They may feel the new work will take you away from the time you can spend with them. Be cautious of possible ridicule from this area. If you want to retain these friends, ignore their negative reactions to your decision. Understand their motives. They may not be aware of them, themselves.

If you have a good extended family and if you want them to be on your side you can accomplish this through patience and understanding on your part. Listen to them. They may be right. They know you and love you. Make them listen to you. Plan to include them. Think of the problems which might occur because of the career selection and try to minimize them through understanding and planning You must also have a good understanding of the new career or careers you are considering so that you can explain the reasons for the choice to others.

160

Chapter 15
Putting Off Until Tomorrow What You Can

How to Do It All

I am asked, over and over, "How do you do it all?" The answer is that I don't do it all, all of the time. I do enough of everything some of the time so that everything seems to be done most of the time and there is no revolution at home or at work. Is that clear? Probably not, but a little confusion makes for an interesting day. If you keep everything too clear and in too rigid a pattern, everyone will notice if you don't get something done.

If I had not put off a few things, and probably more than a few things over the years, I would not have written any of my books or any number of other things I have written. I would not have opened my own law practice. I would not have painted any pictures or taken any photographs because all of these things were, in a sense, not absolutely necessary. These were not things I had to do as part of my responsibilities.

These were things that I liked to do. They brought pleasure to my days and pride to both myself and my family. They are not in the same class as doing the wash and scrubbing the floor or cleaning the oven. I do not like to wash or scrub floors although I do like the resulting cleanliness. I don't even like to talk about cleaning the oven, although I do love to cook. I do like to write and paint. Many people have considered these an absolute waste of my time. None of these things are guaranteed sources of income. If they had been, it might have given these people some justification under the puritanical code which still controls many lives. They were, however, important to me. Somehow I managed to keep my family in clean clothes and have the house relatively straightened up while doing the things which I considered more important.

I have posted a little hand-painted ceramic magnet on my refrigerator door which I bought at a county fair in New England years ago. I am certain that heads must have turned as I bought the piece because I was laughing so hard. The inscription describes the way I work at times. It says, "If it weren't for the last minute, a lot of things wouldn't get done."

I'm afraid that is true many times in my life. It isn't always a matter of procrastination, however. It is a matter of becoming comfortable with planning things and planning them right down to the wire. Last Minute Management is my term for this way of proceeding. You will need to learn how to do this if you are going to make the changes in your life that are necessary for your new career.

162

It is amazing how much time you actually cannot account for in your day. People who have to charge their time to accounts, like attorneys, accountants, and people who work on government contracts, quickly become aware of this. If only we could get back some of those idly spent hours. The next section will discuss the management of your time and the way to squeeze a little extra from each day. If you are going to actually accomplish the career change you have selected, you will have to begin putting something off until tomorrow so that you can work on other things today.

Starting Your Personal Program

Identify the things you must change in yourself and start a personal program for them.

Exercise 15.1

List ten things on your personal program for change.

1 _____
2 _____
3 _____
4 _____
5 _____
6 _____
7 _____
8 _____
9 _____
10 _____

163

Do they involve physical fitness, grooming, new clothes, or improving your speech? How soon can you get started to improve these things? How about riding your bicycle before dinner, jogging before breakfast, or a set of grammar lessons on tape that can be played in the car to and from your present job? What will you put off to do these things, a few minutes sleep, or listening to your favorite radio station. See what you can squeeze in if you think about it! Take a look at your list. How long will it take you to accomplish these things? Write in an amount of time next to each item on your list. If you have put down long time periods such as years; break down these accomplishments into smaller pieces. How little time can you allot to doing these things and still get something done? How much time can you give?

Identify the educational training you must obtain in order to prepare for your new career. Map a schedule to obtain this training. Do you need refresher courses, or are you starting from the beginning in your program? Do you have the prerequisite courses? How long will it take you? Don't procrastinate with respect to finding out these details. Put yourself on a schedule at least to investigate these questions. You may have to put some other things off until tomorrow but it will be worth it in the end.

Have you decided on an educational program you are going to follow? Where will you get these courses? How much will they cost? How often are they given? At what time are they given? A complete study of this program will be discussed in a later chapter. Here you are only trying to get an idea of managing your time so that you can start your program.

Do you have a resume to write and a set of inquiry letters to type? Get that rough draft finished. Have a friend review it for you. Find a good typist if your own fingers can't reproduce the necessary flawless quality which is needed. Using the computer or word processor will help you do this yourself. There are some business supply places and photocopy places that offer a resume service. They will type out your resume on a computer and print as many copies as you need. You keep the disk that contains the resume and, for a small fee, they will make changes that you need at a later time. You won't have to have your resume completely retyped every time you have a new accomplishment.

Exercise 15.2

What two things can you start today or at least this week. How big a time period can you set aside to do this. Will you have to eliminate something to do it? Can you set aside fifteen or twenty minutes?

1_____

2_____

Finding Quality Time

Although there are many things you must put off, do not put off spending time with your family. Your children will only be young once and that time can never be reclaimed. You will also have to be conscious of the needs of your spouse or other family members. There are a lot of books written about positive time spent with family. You may

think that it is family time when you are doing your chores because you are doing things for them but they most likely will not see it that way. They will want your undivided attention part of the time, at least. They will want you to do things with them as well. Involve your family in what you are doing. You will want to minimize any negative feelings which they will have about the career choice. They may fear that the new career will take you away from them. Don't begin by spending all of your time preparing for the new career. Realize, however, that they may be selfish. You have to analyze their demands and see what is reasonable. You will have to achieve the balance yourself and the hardest thing of all may be convincing them.

The things you decide to put off should be explained to your family and close friends if they are affected in some manner. Perhaps you will have to hire someone to do some of the jobs which you are going to have to postpone in order to reach your new goal. This might be a wise investment of both time and money, even if money is a problem. You can't be in more than two places at the same time! Did I say two? Sometimes it seems that the number is far greater than two if you are to respond to all the demands made on you.

Remember that procrastination can be a good thing if it is planned with care and does not just happen. The key to everything is the management of your time.

Equality is a word for our century. No one in days gone by thought of or dreamed of equality. Even among those who may have desired it, few thought that it was possible. Every person is an individual. We differ in size, in color, in sex, in intelligence, in wealth, in talent, in power, and in beauty. The list could go on forever, it seems. These things cannot be made equal in any two individuals. Not only are there the natural limitations, there is also the lack of a standard. For example, the concept of beauty differs not only with culture and background, but also with personal taste. The only real equality is the equality of time.

Every person–rich, poor, brilliant, insane, beautiful, ugly, happy, sad–has the same amount of time in a day. The length of our lives may vary, but in each day we have the same amount of time. My husband brought home a little hand-painted wooden plaque few months ago that says "Once upon a time, there was enough time." We set it up by our computer just to remind us of the truth of that statement.

Time Management: A Problem and a Solution

The question of time management is a serious one in the industrial setting. There are a number of time-management workshops devoted to this. High-level executives must organize their time so that their company gets the maximum benefit from their activities. Before a plan can be developed, the executive, often in cooperation with a time management expert, analyzes the activities that take up his day. Things like phone calls and answering the mail are closely documented on a worksheet. After a clear picture of the range of daily activities is documented, a plan for better management of that. time is created. Together, we will carry out a similar study on the ways you spend your time and create a personal time-management plan for you. This will include time for you to work on things that you must do to provide for the new career while still maintaining your current position and life commitments.

I always remember the movie "Cheaper by the Dozen" when I think of time management. The movie, a charming family comedy, was made from the autobiography with the same title written by Frank Gilbreth, Jr. the eldest son of the twelve children of Frank and Lillian Gilbreth. These two individuals are often credited with initiating the concept of time and motion studies and time management. The movie and book contain delightful scenes of the father studying the children's pattern of brushing teeth, taking baths and dressing. The mother, a very warm individual with certain expected burdens as the mother of twelve children, assisted him in his studies. She took her husband's place when he died suddenly on the way to present his theories at a European conference. In days long before women's lib, she became an important figure in the development of modern theories of business. The analysis of your daily life according to time spent may seem as foolish as the analysis of the brushing of the Gilbreth children's teeth. Please be certain that it is not. Time is even more precious than money. There is no return policy for time. You definitely can only spend time once. Even if you realize that you wasted it, you can never get it back. We must make certain that those things which are really important to you are included in your time management program along with those things which you are obligated to do.

Where Did the Time Go?

The very first question to be answered is "What do you do with your day?" If I ask you this question, you will probably be able to tell me what has happened to large blocks of your time. You drove to work, ate lunch, went to a meeting, and cooked dinner. You may be surprised to discover how much time you cannot account for. It may add up to a considerable percentage of your day. If you do this analysis, don't show it to your boss. He or she may not realize how much time you are not able to account for. Because you cannot account for it does not mean that you are wasting the time. It really means that the manner in which the time was spent was not important enough to you for you to be able to recall it.

Managing Your Own Time

The secret of time management is to spend your time more effectively, that is, to spend more of your time on things that are important to you.

In order to manage your time, you will first have to do a study of where it is going.

Exercise 15.3

Now for a long range assignment. Get a notebook which you can keep rather inconspicuously in your pocket or handbag and jot down all the waking hours in a day and what you do during those hours. If your days seem to be pretty much alike then do it for two weekdays and both weekend days. If they are different, do it for a little longer period. It may be obvious to you when you write down your time expenditure just where you can pick up a little more time. Or you may be frightened by the number of things you manage to accomplish in a day. If you are already doing a great deal, doing a few more things won't matter. The saying "If you need something done, give it to a busy person."

Exercise 15.4

Next, set aside time allotments for the tasks which you need to perform. The things you need to accomplish to prepare yourself for your new career may be only a few tasks or the list may include a great many items. You may have to read through books on different careers. You have all of the exercises that were set out in the other chapters. You have to spend time on the *Dictionary of Occupational Titles*. You have to develop a resume and inquiry letters. You have to look through professional journals in a career area in which you are interested and then sort current jobs that are mentioned in these magazines. You have to identify the abilities you will have to show to in order to qualify for one of these jobs. You have to establish computer skills and learn to use the Internet.

168

Break these tasks down into small pieces and estimate the time you would need to accomplish them.

1 _____
2 _____
3 _____
4 _____
5 _____
6 _____
7 _____
8 _____
9 _____
10 _____

"I don't really have time to do these things," you might be telling yourself. Do you have fifteen minutes a day to spend? "What can I do in fifteen minutes", you will surely be asking. For example, fifteen minutes might be enough time to work on one section of your resume. It might be enough time to type a brief inquiry letter or prepare several envelopes. It would be sufficient time to study the classified ads in most newspapers. Papers like the New York Times always take a little longer but they offer so much more. Fifteen minutes of exercise or attention to grooming could fulfill some part of a personal appearance development program which you have worked out for yourself. You might be surprised at what you could do with fifteen minutes if you deliberately set aside that time to work on a specific project every day.

Exercise 15.5

Write down ten things that you can accomplish in fifteen minutes.

1 _____
2 _____
3 _____
4 _____
5 _____
6 _____
7 _____
8 _____
9 _____
10 _____

Many of the things which you will want to accomplish cannot be done in such short time periods, I realize. They can still be completed in reasonably small units. You say that it will take four years to complete your degree or perhaps even more if you are only able to attend part time. But that will not mean every minute for four years. How many courses and how many hours per session and how many sessions per week will you need to take? These are the questions which you will have to answer. How many hours of homework for each hour of class will you have to spend on the average? Knowing this you will be able to make a plan or schedule for yourself. What did you do with the last four years? If you had started then, you might be finished now. Since you can't start any sooner, start now.

How do you schedule an evening class into your life? You do, that's all. Don't expect it to just happen, you have to make plans for it. You may have to temporarily eliminate something else. It may mean that you will have to postpone bowling, Monday Night Football or an evening soap opera. Something may have to go in order to have enough available time to get something done. The thing you have to do is to establish priorities in your life. Priorities don't exist in the same order forever. If the important thing for you is to prepare for your new career, you have to overlay the time expenditure for that against the daily schedule you cannot alter. Make your immediate time plan and, if necessary, make a long-range time plan as well. Evaluate your daily expenditures of time, penciling some items in and postponing others. Are there some things you enjoy doing that must be postponed?

Do you spend time doing things which you do not want to do, so that they take up all your available time? Many people who are caught in this pattern don't realize that they are doing it. Pretend you are working for yourself. Think of a task which you don't like to do. Would you pay yourself to do that task? Would you pay yourself for the number of minutes or hours it took you to do it? Or would you have fired yourself for being too slow? This is a way in which you can check up on yourself. Are you spending too much of that valuable time on tasks which you could be doing in significantly less time? Is one of the reasons the fact that you are not being paid for this time? You may not cheat on your boss's time in the same fashion as you are cheating on your own time. The reason is that your boss is paying you. The solution is to pay yourself. Reward yourself with the time saved and do something you like to do in the time saved. Who wants to rush scrubbing the floor if your reward is having the time to clean the oven. You will get more done than if you had to spend the whole time doing the tasks you hate to do and being caught in the puritanical loop of feeling guilty because you are not working. That is why you initially drag out tasks you dislike. You will find that as you are able to get your tasks done in a smaller amount of time, you can begin to direct the time saved to move you toward your new career.

While you are rearranging your schedule, don't eliminate everything that you enjoy because that will depress you too much. Finding a new career is a stressful activity and you will need to have some enjoyment left in your life while you are making that change. Are there patterns of wasted time in your life which need to be broken? Are you living a rash expenditure of time? Your need to work your way out of procrastination may be the answer.

Chapter 16
Catching Up with Time

Time Will Not Stand Still

Perhaps the most devastating discovery for a person who is changing to a new career is that time did not stand still for him or her. Although it seems rather arrogant to express the expectation in those terms, and few will do so explicitly, many individuals seem to expect this to be the case. It is most dramatically seen in the case of those who have not worked for a number of years. This is particularly true for women who have good educations. They return to the work force after a number of years of absence and expect to be paid as though they had been working and gaining experience during the intervening years. The person who has been working in another area expects to be paid for the experience he/she gained in that other area. Neither of these people may have experience in regard to their new career. This presents a difficult consideration for both the person who is going to hire these people as well as for the job seeker. For many, it is a very bitter adjustment to realize that the years which have passed may not count at all or at least count very little toward seniority in the new position.

This situation is very difficult to face. The solution lies in compromise, maximization of preparation, and adjustment.

It is important that the person entering a new career be aware of the pressures on the person who is doing the hiring. This will minimize potential bitter feelings and disappointment. A young person starting out in a first career may want to begin with the same income and lifestyle that his or her parents have reached after years of work. With the advances in salaries achieved in the technical areas, this may actually may be possible. Cost-of-living raises have been competing with entering wages in many areas in such a manner that new employees are sometimes paid almost the same as people who have been in the field for a long while. To the new person entering the field this may not seem true but it is the reality in many cases. This arouses bitterness in some individuals who have been working within a field for a number of years, and this attitude on the part of fellow workers will also have to be faced. Inflation is destroying not only our ability to buy but also our ability to gain some kind of credit for work performance.

174   Gaining Credit for Your Past Experience

The person entering a new career must make every effort to gain maximum credit for his or her past experiences. They must face the factor of time very consciously.

There are some negative aspects to time. Time has made us grow older. In a world that puts youth on a pedestal, we may feel less attractive than when we were younger although it is possible for us to actually be more attractive. Some consider thirty to be young while for others it is ancient. Both the person who is changing careers and the person who is starting out with a first career must present an attractive image. Image is more than appearance, although the way you look is an important part of your image.

Time should have made us wiser, yet many people may be out of date in a particular field or with respect to a particular skill. There will be a need to evaluate required skills or preparation. Although not all fields have changed drastically, no field has stood still in the past few years. If you were trained for a specific career, you will have to assess where you stand with respect to current knowledge and present practice in your chosen field. You will also have to discover a way to upgrade your skills or learn new ones. How can you demonstrate your abilities? How can you convince a prospective employer that you are capable of functioning to his or her standard in your new career? These questions are equally valid if you are just starting out in a career or if you are changing careers. How do you get the experience you need if all the available jobs require experience? Catch 22.

Time should have made us more secure in our interactions with other individuals. When entering a new career, however, an individual who has many years of work experience, may feel as insecure as a young person taking his or her first job.

There are many questions you will be faced with.

- How can you gain the necessary new poise and security?
- How can you show confidence which you may not necessarily feel?
- How can you translate skills learned in a previous job into a new work area?
- How can you work with or for people who may be much younger than you are?
- How can you work with or for people who are not as bright as you are?
- How can you work with or for people who do not have the latest training as you have?

These are only a few of the questions you will have to consider in advance of any change you may make.

Although you will certainly try to maximize your opportunities, you may find yourself reporting to a younger person. Your attitude towards your supervisor will be as important to your success as his or her attitude toward you. You had better be aware of this possible conflict beforehand. Time did not stand still for you, but the intervening years do not count for as much as you may have estimated. This may require a severe adjustment on your part. It may be necessary for you to accept the situation, at least on a temporary basis. Do not be ashamed. It does not represent failure on your part. It is a fact of life that time does not stand still.

Evaluating Yourself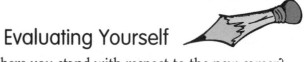

How can you evaluate where you stand with respect to the new career?

How can you boost your starting place on the career ladder?

How can you turn back the clock?

How can you make time stand still?

The answer is that you can't, but you can try to compensate for it.

Self-evaluation is always difficult. Some individuals are able to objectively view themselves, but they are very few in number. Most people have managed to remain unaware of their faults and to cover up their weaknesses. These individuals have a far more difficult time in setting their skills in proper perspective. They find themselves possessing the attitude "Why don't they realize how wonderful I am?"

Few people will realize how wonderful you are. You will have to convince them with your performance. Unfortunately, life is not always fair and the talents of many people are not recognized. If you are going to make up the lost years, you will have to carefully plan the steps needed to reach the next position on your chosen career ladder.

Other sections of this book will discuss creating your image and improving your skills. Here we will discuss identifying the characteristics of your present career and life that will support your new career.

Techniques for Transfer of Training

What you must do is develop the concept of transferring the training which you had in your old career, job, volunteer work or organizational activity over to your new career. In simple terms, the transfer concept states that what you have learned about specific ways of performing some activity from one job, you can transfer (carry over) to the new job. When you do this analysis the kind of things that have been transferred will be clearer to you. You are trying to convince your prospective employer and perhaps yourself that you have actual experience in certain areas because of characteristics of work you have done in the past. If your experiences are limited, or if you have not worked in a while, you may find yourself stretching the point a little, but this is still a valuable exercise. You will use the information you develop in both writing your resume and in your interviews to make this analysis. To do this you will have to learn the tasks you will be performing in the new job in detail. You may also use it to convince yourself that you do indeed have some preparation for the new position. If you are able to identify a substantial number of tasks in which you are already competent, you will gain added confidence in your ability to do the new job. If you cannot find many similar tasks, you will have to realize that you may have to start pretty close to the bottom in your new area.

In order to do this evaluation effectively, you will have to thoroughly study the new career and, in particular, the entry level positions in that career. What will you have to do or know in the first job you get in this career ladder? What would be the characteristics of the second position, the third, etc.?

If you have problems identifying types of characteristics, take a look at the headings in the *Dictionary of Occupational Titles*. Remember the book with over 20,000 job entries? Remember all those headings and characteristics associated with different jobs? Remember working with people, data, and things? You have thought about the characteristics of the new career. What are they?

Take a piece of paper and rule off a number of columns and rows. In the first few columns place the names of the positions in the first few jobs in your new chosen career field. Place the names of other jobs you have held or volunteer activities you have directed and your educational experiences over the other columns. Under the new career columns, list the characteristics associated with your new area. Under the other headings, list the characteristics which were associated with your other positions in the same rows. Match up the characteristics. How many do you already have, even if the job titles are not the same? Under education, list those things you have learned that will support the new position.

Exercise 16.1

Job characteristics	New job	Previous job	Next previous job
1			
2			
3			
4			
5			
6			
7			
8			
9			
10			

Have you thought about the characteristics of your old jobs? They don't even have to be characteristics which you particularly liked. You are trying to build up a portfolio of supportive experiences.

178

Exercise 16.2

Now write down the job characteristics of the last three jobs you had, or the most relevant jobs you have held. Check off some of the characteristics of your old jobs that are part of the new jobs for which you are preparing yourself.

Job characteristics	Job1	Job2	Job3
1			
2			
3			
4			
5			
6			
7			
8			
9			
10			

Are there things listed under the old job columns which will support the new career? Are there items which you can use as evidence that you have done things similar to those required by the new career?

The more characteristics you can find among your old jobs to support your new career, the better evidence you have that you should not have to start on the first rung of the new ladder. The chances will be better for you to start at a more advanced position, as well as actually being able to perform the tasks required in the new position.

If you have not worked for a long time, you will have to pull together some of the characteristics of the volunteer activities in which you have engaged. Stretch your ideas, but don't get ridiculous. Driving children to baseball practice does not necessarily prepare you to be a Director of Transportation. Running a major charity drive, however, does give you excellent experience in organizing details and managing people. If you have not had a great deal of paid work experience, or if your jobs have been selected just to sustain yourself while you are going through school, you may not have many entries and may have to put in the characteristics of volunteer activity you have performed. Remember, the person who hires you will have to answer to someone else and explain why he or she though you were qualified for the new position. You have to understand these answers for yourself and give them to the person who interviews you.

Let us suppose you have done your homework. You have related your past experiences to the demands of the new job. You have improved your skills in the new area, you have worked on your image and done all the things you need to do. You will still have to adjust yourself to the fact that unless something extraordinary happens you will not be given full credit for all your working years. This is especially the case for those years in which you have not worked for a salary. Do not believe that you will not be given any credit for those years but it will be up to you to demonstrate that you deserve this credit.

No one could ever convince me that staying home to raise a family is not work, but many people do not regard it that way. Although homemaking is definitely work, it may be that there are not many characteristics associated with it that can be transferred to the new career area and represented as countable experience. Many women who have good educations, worked for a few years and then dropped out to take care of their families, are very resentful when they are placed in an entry level career position. If you have done everything you can think of to maximize your position, you may have to adjust your thinking. You may have to accept the role of beginner once more.

If you are not able to convince a potential employer that you are entitled to consideration for past experience in non-related work, it is possible that you will still be able to move up more quickly in the new position than a younger person could. Maturity does count for something. It's up to you to make that happen.

Beginning in the right place is important but so is getting promoted. You will have to show your new employer that those past years were not wasted and that you have the skills needed to move you along at a faster rate than your younger colleagues.

180   Identify the reasons that people get promoted within your new career position. What are the characteristics needed for the next promotion? Would more education be of assistance? Do you dress, act and perform as though you are in your next position already? Reinforcing your own belief in yourself will help you to catch up with time.

Chapter 17
Creating the New Image

Recognizing the Image Others Have of You

I had a wonderful great-aunt who lived to be ninety-nine years old. The difference in our ages was such that I can only remember her as "old". While to me she was old all of my life, she never considered herself to be old. When she reached her eighties she would joke about approaching middle age. Her mind was bright and her memory good until she died. She always had health problems but she kept going. In the days I knew her, she was not glamorous, she was comfortable. A tiny woman, she was bosomy. When she hugged you, you felt the warmth and love which was her essence. A few years before she died, we had a talk about the person inside the body.

"You know," I said, "I don't feel any older than when I was in high school. I forget sometimes until I look in a mirror." She smiled at me. "I know how you feel," she said. "I don't believe it either. I don't know how I got to be so old. I don't even realize just how old I am until I pass a mirror. I look in and say to myself, 'Who is that old lady there? Where did she come from?' Then I realize that it is me. I never thought I would ever get to be so old. I never feel I am so old."

We smiled together each knowing that the other felt the same although we were separated by a lifetime of years.

Do you recognize the face in the mirror? Does the image others have of you resemble the image you have of yourself? If you are going to start a new career, possibly a new lifestyle, and maybe even change your whole life, you may have to begin with a change in your image. The life you want to have may require you to create a new image for yourself. You will certainly have to consider your images and evaluate them. Notice I said images.

An image may be defined as a mental picture. There are many images of YOU. Do you know what they are? Whether you want to create a new image or are happy with the old one, you will have to examine these images from different points of view. At the very least, you must consider your own view, that of those who know you, and the view of those who are just meeting you. While you might consider the one who interviews you for a job to be too conservative, too old-fashioned, or too sloppy, you will have to accommodate yourself to the image of the industry you are trying to enter. Technical areas have always been more liberal about manner of dress and length of hair than other areas but there is no need to try and push the envelope. You might do well to listen to your mother about getting that haircut or not wearing your skirt so short. I'm not saying it is necessary but think about it.

Exercise 17.1

Write down the components of the image you believe you are currently projecting. Include any aspect of your image that you believe is your present projection.

1 _____
2 _____
3 _____
4 _____
5 _____
6 _____
7 _____
8 _____
9 _____
10 _____

Because this book is for both men and women, you might think I would have to write a separate section for each sex. After all, men are not interested in advice on the length of a skirt nor are women concerned with the pattern of a tie. This is not the case, however. The question of image is so much larger than the details of skirt length and tie pattern that there is no need to distinguish according to sex. It may even be useful to know some of the things that must be considered by individuals of the opposite sex when they are creating their own images. Your image is a creation linking many components. One of them is your physical appearance.

What Are Your Physical Characteristics?

First, let us consider your physical appearance. Included in this is the question of your physical health, your physical well-being as well as your physical characteristics. How would others describe your physical characteristics? How do you describe yourself?

We have all had to fill in those questions on applications about sex and height and weight, color of hair and eyes, etc. These answers are part of your physical image. Age and possibly race may be asked on some forms although there are times when employers are restricted by law from asking such questions.

Think a moment about these physical characteristics. Remember, I do not mean just appearance now. That will be our next discussion.

Exercise 17.2

Let's get out the pencil and paper again and write down the answers to some questions.

Age
Weight
Height
Color of hair
Race
Waist measurement
Hip measurement
Bust(chest to measurement

You don't have to let anyone see you doing this and you can burn your answers if you are afraid someone might find them in the wastebasket.

How did you answer these questions? What did you write down for your age? What is your birth date? Subtract your birth date from today's date. Did you write down the right age for yourself? If you are young, or old, you probably did. If you are somewhere in the middle you may not have written the correct figure. I must admit I sometimes have trouble myself unless I do a little subtraction. If you do not want to think of yourself as being your correct age, how old do you want others to think you are? Is this realistic? If you are forty, no one is going to think you are twenty. You might try for thirty-five, if that is important to you. The same may be even more true if you are older.

What did you write down for your weight? Go into the bathroom and get on the scale. You can take your shoes off if it will make you feel better. Is there more than a five pound difference between what you wrote down and what the scale revealed? Think about this.

184

You may be the correct weight for your age and height, or you may be too thin or too heavy. All scales may be your enemy, but it is important that you be aware of your weight. I am not suggesting that you change your weight, only that you be aware of it yourself.

The current American fad is to be thin and this is reflected in those proper weight charts that you find in diet books. What do you think your weight should be? It will vary according to your age. Does the chart you are using take age and sex into consideration? How close are you to the so-called correct weight for your age and height? If you are very far off, are you content with your weight? If you want to change your weight, is there some realistic intermediate goal that you could set? If you are thinking of going on a diet, you should discuss it first with your doctor.

Now I want you to get out the measurement tape and check your body dimensions. Are you close to what you wrote down? In addition to the waist measurement, men should measure about one inch above the belt. Are you still quoting that old waist measurement and thinking that you are just as you were when you were in high school or college when you are really hanging over your belt?

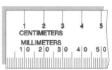

Do these measurements please you? Are there changes you would like to make?

You have written down some values, discovered the true values, and made some estimates of what you would really like these figures to be. It is important that you be realistic. If you are no longer young, you should not select figures for your goals that are appropriate for a teenager. Try and work out a set of figures for yourself that are right for you.

You may want to think about some kind of exercise program for yourself. Not only might this improve your measurements, but it might be very good for your general health and energy level. Again you should be certain to check with your physician before beginning such a program. The same exercise is not right for everyone. What kind of exercise can you fit into your lifestyle? Begin slowly and gradually increase your commitment to exercise. There are many gyms now as well as private groups and adult education classes, that focus on improving yourself through exercise. There are machines you can have in your home which you can use to exercise certain parts of your body. Jogging and aerobics have both become important techniques for exercise. Walking, both regular walking and fast walking, improves the cardiovascular response as well as burning calories. More people are engaging in sports than ever before. Tennis, golf, and in-line skating are all examples of individual sports that can give you some exercise as well as enjoyment. There are even exercises that can be done sitting down.

185

What changes would you like to make in the characteristics you wrote down? I would like to be taller than my height of five feet, but I cannot do much about that. I would like to be younger but that's out of my hands also. If the number of diets printed in the monthly magazines means anything, I am not alone in my desire to be thinner. Although that always seems to elude me, I am still working on that phase of my image. Is there anything about your physical characteristics that you would like to change?

Health is a factor that must be given strong attention when one is considering a change in career and a possible change in lifestyle. If you remember the Holmes-Rahe Scale which appeared in the first chapter, considerable stress is encountered for a number of reasons when such a change takes place. I have already indicated that you should consult your doctor if you are going to go on a diet. If you are going to be able to survive physically, I recommend that you have a good physical checkup before beginning any major program of change. You may first want to give yourself a kind of mental once over as well.

Do you have any health problems that you have been neglecting or ignoring? Are you feeling good or are you dragged out? Do you experience shortness of breath or extreme weariness at times? How is your vision and your hearing? Depression can have serious effects on your health and you may have experienced some sense of "the blues" lately. If you have some doubts about anything, have a complete checkup. You should also try and be aware of your health as you go through this process. You may experience some changes in your health —for better or for worse. Be aware of these changes and respond with good sense.

Your health is often shown through some of your physical characteristics. The shine (or dullness) of your hair, the condition of your nails, the expression in your eyes and the tone of your skin can all reflect your state of health. Posture is extremely important. Although poor posture may only be the result of bad habits, it also may keep you from being admitted to the executive class. Posture is not fatal but it does detract from the image. Poor posture can make you look sloppy.

Many top executives, both men and women, carry out a regular program of physical fitness. This has several effects. People who exercise regularly find that they feel better. Exercise is good for them physically, it improves their appearance, and it gives them something to talk about at lunch.

Think about some of your other physical habits. I happen to think that smoking, for example, is bad for you and bad for those around you. If you smoke, how compulsive a habit is it? Might it keep you from getting a certain position? What do you

186

look like when you smoke? Many jobs are advertised only for non-smokers. Will you be able to qualify? If your clothing smells of smoke, you will hardly be able to convince a prospective employer that you are a non-smoker. Places that hire only non-smokers don't want to hire smokers who won't smoke on the premises but are constantly running down to the parking lot to have a cigarette.

Do you drink much? Think about this honestly. Does it affect your appearance? Is it affecting your health or family relationships? Drugs, like alcohol, are a destructive component of many lives. You may instantly say that you don't take drugs, but consider those drugs prescribed by your physician. Do you, for example, take tranquilizers or sleeping pills? There have been a number of articles written lately concerning drug habits which began with physician-prescribed medications. Years ago, Betty Ford, the former first lady, made some courageous and revealing statements about this problem, which caused a number of doctors and patients to regulate their medications. Be aware of yourself. Do your best to take care of your health.

I do not mean, in any way, to discourage anyone who has a health problem or a physical handicap from considering making a career change. It is certainly as important and as possible for you as it is for anyone else. You are probably aware of the status of your health and will work with that factor in setting your new goals. What I am trying to say is that health is very important and many people are not aware of the dynamic role that health plays in any kind of change.

187

Others, both those who know you well and those who are just meeting you, may be more aware of your physical characteristics than you are. After all, you don't go around looking at yourself all the time.

Note that although I am making a distinction between your physical characteristics and your appearance, they are related.

Changing Your Appearance

How do you appear to yourself? How do you appear to others? What do you see when you look in the mirror? What do others see? There are many components to a person's appearance. Such things as dress, hair, shoes, makeup (in the case of women) and accessories are all contributing factors to appearance. These can be carefully calculated to make certain impressions. Other factors such as speech, posture and personal habits, also make significant contributions to the overall impression you make. These elements are more difficult to change and will require that you work out a program for changing yourself. Let us look at each of these elements individually.

Dress

Clothes make the man (or woman), as they say. Although some people claim they do not have the time, money or interest to dress in a certain way, they cannot deny that clothes are a very large part of their appearance and play a role in creating an impression.

Thomas Watson, the founder of IBM, was very much aware of this factor and set criteria for the attire of his salesmen, including white

188 shirts, that remained a standard in industry for many years. The distinction between the white-collared worker and the blue-colored worker was not an accident of speech. Although today colored shirts are accepted in every profession, the white shirt is still the standard against which the others are measured.

You should dress not for the job you have, but for the job you want to have. That is a useful goal to keep before you especially if you are entering a new career.

Your clothes are an important part of your image. A number of books have focused on attire for the executive woman and/or the executive man. *The Woman's Dress For Success* Book by John T. Molloy, (Warner Books, 1976), which became a best seller, used a scientific approach to discover the type of clothes that would be most successful for the career woman. He found that the most successful uniform for a career mobile woman was a skirted suit and blouse. The suit would be most effective in a color such as medium blue, gray, camel, beige, black or brown, and should be worn with a contrasting blouse. Black was somewhat inhibiting. I found the book interesting, did some adjustment in my own wardrobe, and began making observations at professional meetings. I found that others had begun to read books such as these and that number included the buyers in the department stores. I was suddenly able to purchase suitable clothing without having to go to very exclusive stores. One store I frequent now has a corner for executive women which carries a limited number of appropriate fashions. There was indeed a new preponderance of suits at the meetings I attended and the women wearing them looked professional. Not all of the women's suits were in men's clothing colors. Red is a very popular color for women's suits, even among lawyers. I might note that there is a new wave of resistance to wearing suits and the "everyone-now-looks-alike" syndrome. Suits in more feminine styles are beginning to appear. Although there is no law that women must wear a suit or a conservative dress, it is safer to do so. If you feel confident, then you can vary your wardrobe considerably. A safe rule of thumb is that you should stand out only for the attractiveness of your clothing rather than the extremeness unless you are in either the fashion or the entertainment industry.

Molloy's book for women has been matched by a number of books for men which help them learn how to dress in their quest for success. While Mallory's book is more than twenty years out of date now, there are many aspects of dress discussed there which are relevant. Your library may have a copy of the Molloy book for you to review for techniques although the actual styles are certainly out of date. On second thought, they may be recycling into fashion again. It seems that there are only so many styles and these recycle after so many years.

The directions for male attire are similar to those for women if you replace the words "skirted suit" with the word suit. Conservative colors and cuts are always the best choice. Obviously red has limited appeal for men unless your new career is that of Santa Claus. You should be in fashion and fashionable without being guilty of following the latest fad. Loud plaids, checks and very baggy or very tight pants are generally frowned upon, as are loud ties or socks. Individuality has its place, but conservative colors are safe. Again, dress for the job you want to have.

Dressing for success does not always mean dressing conservatively. A photographer I know is a quiet, conservative, mother of three small children married quiet happily to a very handsome male model who gives her great assistance with the children. When she dressed casually and conservatively, she had few jobs, although her photography was outstanding. She had her hair bleached almost white and cut in a very extreme short cut, perhaps only an inch in length. She changed her wardrobe to very extreme and flamboyant clothing. She is completely booked all of the time  now and is very successful in her work, which is primarily fashion photography although the stunning photographs she takes were equally stunning before the change . Whatever the reason for her new success, it was partly caused by her catching the eye of the designers and that was impossible in her plain shirts and jeans.

Women in particular have to be aware of the role they are seeking to play. If you want to be a business executive, then you should not dress in a fashion designed to highlight you as a sex object.

This does not mean that you should not try to be attractive. If you study successful people you will find they are generally very attractive. They may not be naturally pretty or handsome but they have a certain quality about themselves that is quietly pleasing. Note the word quietly. Loud clothes, on men or women, are generally not the road to success. Clothes should be coordinated in color and in style. Although some designers mix colors and patterns that do not usually seem to go together, you must remember they are doing it to create an effect. Sometimes this is so they will be noticed. You, as a professional, do not want to be noticed for unusual, clashing outfits.

The cost of clothing is a serious consideration, but there are many ways around this. Your clothes should never look as though they came from the discount store. This does not mean that they don't come from such a store, it just means that they shouldn't look it. There are several criteria to use. Some of these will change with the years, but in general they remain effective. Good tailoring is important in clothing for both men and women. If there are threads hanging from seams and shoulders or collars don't fit well, the tailoring is poor. The clothes you buy should hang well on you,

190

being neither loose nor tight. Invest in a full-length mirror and model your clothes at home before you wear them. You may even want to take pictures of yourself in various outfits to see the image you are projecting. A digital camera can give you instant feedback on the way you look.

Look in the fashion magazines and in the more expensive stores. Study the clothes that are being sold there. What is the size of the lapel on the men's jackets, how many buttons, what is the style of the waistbands and cuff length this year? What is the style of the women's dresses and suits? What are the lengths? What are the popular colors and fabrics? What examples of fashion can be translated into garments that are appropriate for your new profession? Remember your goal is to have clothing that is fashionable, but projects an appropriate businesslike image.

If your budget is somewhat limited, find yourself one of those super discount places that discount name-brand merchandise. Some of these places do not let you return anything so bring a friend with you. I have my favorite places to buy clothes and shoes. I find that by careful shopping I can save almost 50 percent on my wardrobe and still have the latest appropriate fashion. Quite often I can tell the brand name even if the label is cut out. A number of fine brands have opened their own stores in malls that specialize in outlet stores. It has been very profitable for the manufacturers, but it also is very beneficial for the customers as well.

Anyone who wants to check labels in my clothes is going to be disappointed since many of them were cut out before I bought them. I go to the regular store first and determine price and style. Then I go to my favorite places and often find the same merchandise at thirty to fifty percent off. My husband has his favorite places, also, and shops the same way. Because we travel a lot, we have identified a number of outlets in different parts of the country that are on our "good places to shop" list. We share names with our friends and tip each other off when we learn of a good sale. It is possible to have a very good-looking wardrobe for less than you are spending now, if you shop carefully and efficiently. Don't buy an item because it is a bargain. Will the garment integrate into your wardrobe? Is the color good for you? Will you have to loose ten pounds for it to look right on you? Develop you own list of questions.

You should have certain colors predominate in your wardrobe. When you buy a suit, think of the coordinating blouse or shirt and tie that will go with it. Coordination is especially important in creating an attractive image. If you have problems with colors or are color blind, have a friend help you coordinate your wardrobe.

A conservative, businesslike image may not be the one you wish to project. At least you may not think so now and indeed it may not be the right one for you. If you want to be a rock star, a kindergarten teacher, a construction engineer or an astronaut you will have to select a wardrobe that reflects a different image from the business professional. People who work in merchandising have a different set of rules than people who work in laboratories, but both must be aware of how they should dress for the job. There are many new careers you might select that would fit into a less conservative category. The key, however, is that the wardrobe should be appropriate for the position you are seeking to get or seeking to keep.

192

Some things you may feel are obvious apparently have been forgotten by individuals I have seen over the years. Clothes should be neat, well-pressed, clean and not show signs of wear, like rings around collars, frayed cuffs, wrinkled jackets and uneven hems. I saw a sign the other day which read "Are wrinkles holding you back in life?" I realized as I looked closer that it was an ad from a dry-cleaners not a company which sold makeup. Think of the people who seem to you to be attractive. What is their image? Would you like to project a similar image? What elements create their image? What changes would you have to make in your appearance to emulate that image?

Again, coordination is an important element. You must look as though you were put together by design and did not just happen. Although some people think women should dress so as to fade into the woodwork, I do not agree with this. Dress for both men and women should never be loud or conspicuous but should be distinctive. Men who are on the way up dress well and attractively. Shirt, tie and suit are coordinated by color and style. Women should follow the same rules. Colors should be coordinated and styles flattering but not sexy or with a hint of being evening wear. Necklines should not be low. Skirts should not be tight or too short.

If you have an important meeting coming up, choose your wardrobe carefully. A digital camera that develops pictures instantly can be used to help you analyze your image. Have someone take a picture of you in the outfit you have chosen. The camera often reveals much more than the mirror. What image does the outfit project? Is it the one you are seeking to create? Does the outfit fit you properly? Is the color good for you?

How Should You Wear Your Hair?

Long or short, curly or straight, natural or dyed, hair, above all should always be clean. The dandruff commercials get to us at times but they do have a valid message. No matter how attractively you are dressed, the effect will be ruined by dandruff on your collar. Hair should be an appropriate length and style. What length is appropriate, you ask? That certainly has varied over the past few years. A woman who wears her hair long will give the image of a little girl. If she is seeking an executive position she is presenting a confusing image. A man who wears his hair long and ties it up in a ponytail is also presenting a different image when he goes seeking a position. A crewcut projects a still different image, which may be as much of a problem as the ponytail on a man in certain situations. Again we have the situation of being "in style" without being too far ahead of the general trend. The fashion magazines are sometimes not much help when it comes to hair. In the women's magazines, at least, hairdos are often wild and not suitable for daily wear. Find a style that is attractive and stay up to date.

How Should You Select Your Shoes?

Shoes, whatever the style, should be polished and have good heels and soles on them. Some feel that women should wear very plain shoes, but I feel an unattractive shoe will take away from an otherwise

193

attractive image. The shoe should not make any sound when you walk. It should not squeak or flip-flop. It should not be an "evening shoe" with heels so high as to be unsteady. Men should not generally wear a work shoe or a heavy boot in an office position. There are always exceptions. The important thing is that you are conscious of the image you are trying to project when you choose your footwear.

What About Glasses?

Glasses are a necessity of life for many and that number used to include me. I used to say that I couldn't find mine without them. This would still be true but I have worn soft contacts for years and I love them. While contacts can be great they are not suitable for everyone.

It always surprises me how many well-groomed, stylish people neglect their eyeglasses. You see people in very attractive outfits with glasses that are discolored, out of style and unflattering. Perhaps some of the trim is missing. They may have marks on their faces from ill-fitting glasses. They keep pushing them back up on their noses because they do not fit properly. I have even seen frames taped together. Your face is the heart of your appearance and your glasses dominate your face. Be certain that they are in good condition, attractive, and up to date. If you have difficulty seeing without your glasses take a friend with you to select frames. It is hard to choose effectively when you can't see.

Selecting Accessories

It always somewhat amazes me that a man can fit into his pockets what a woman needs a piece of luggage to carry. A large purse is out of place for a woman in an executive position. Many carry a briefcase that has a section in it to hold the essentials of life. Instead of carrying many things around with you, keep a second set of certain necessities (cosmetics, toothbrush, extra pantihose) in the office. A man does not

194

enter a meeting looking as though he is on his way to catch a plane with carry-on luggage. A woman should not be dragging a heavy purse in addition to her briefcase. Jewelry should be tastefully chosen and not make excessive noise like dangling charm bracelets. Too much jewelry is not appropriate in a business offices, although this is certainly not true in all cases. The entertainment industry is only one exception. The appropriate briefcase is a considera-tion for both men and women. It must be large enough to handle what is generally carried to meetings and yet not look like a portable steamer trunk. It should usually be made of leather and exude quality. If you carry a day-planner, don't stuff it with notes that will drop out at the first opportunity.

Men must consider their own accessories. A belt should be carefully chosen. Wallet and keys should not make an unsightly bulge in your pocket. Jewelry for men is more acceptable than it used to be but it should be chosen with taste. A good watch and conservative ring are always acceptable.

195

Posture is important

The manner in which your clothing hangs is determined, in part, by your pos-ture. Posture is important and may be something you neglect. Try and view yourself in a triple mirror. Do your shoulders hunch over? Does your derriere stick out? There are exercises you can follow to improve your posture. Not only will you look better, you will feel better. You may need to have a friend give you gentle reminders to straighten up every once in a while. It would be a help to have someone videotape you when you are walking naturally and not aware of the camera. You will probably be more critical about yourself than anyone else would be when you see yourself.

What Are Your Personal habits?

There are a number of personal habits that may interfere with your overall image. Biting your nails or touching your face, hair or nose can be negative actions which are noticed by others. Chewing gum does not look professional. Smoking is not as accepted as it once was and in many places is not permitted. Think of the little habits you may have developed. Make a short list of them. Do they contribute in a positive way to the image you are trying to create? If not, make the decision to eliminate them from your life.

What Impression Do You make on Others?

The impression you make on others is made up of a number of different factors. You will certainly want to make different impressions on different people and in different circumstances. I act differently with my children than I do with my professional colleagues. I dress differently on the weekend than I do on weekdays when I am going to court. When my neighbor sees me getting in the car to go to the tennis courts or to the beach, he certainly gets a different impression of me than when I am either going out for the evening or going to present a technical paper at a meeting or going to court. All of these images are valid. I would certainly wear different clothing for each of these affairs. My hair, my shoes, and my general bearing will be different, although my reaction to meeting him might be the same in all three cases. The impression you make on someone is related to your appearance but is always part of the image you are trying to create.

Whether you are conscious of it or not, you are making an impression on those who meet you. If you are going to create a successful new image, you must be aware of the impression you are creating. It may or may not be the impression you wish to create.

Exercise 17.3

Take your pencil and paper again and write down four or five different situations that you find yourself in quite often. These should be important to you but vary the situation. They might be such things as "meeting people at a party," "making a formal presentation to my superiors," "interviewing for a new position," "working with my peers," "working with my subordinates," "meeting new customers," "teaching something to children," or "meeting new people." Make each of these situations the heading of a column. Under each heading write down three or four of your characteristics that you would like people to be aware of in the situation identified at the heading of the column. For example, I would like my superiors to be aware of my efficiency and my intelligence, but I might like new people I have just met at a party to be aware of my friendliness or attractiveness. My intelligence might or might not be the thing I would like them to be aware of at a first meeting.

There are many ways in which we create certain impressions. Our choice of clothing and our choice of words are certainly very important.

You have identified certain situations in your life and certain impressions you would like to make in each of these. The next time you are in these situations be conscious of the impression you are making. Is it the one you want to make? What could you do to change things so that you do make the impression you desire to make? Be certain that you are being true to yourself. Is the impression you want to create one that is really you? Creating a false impression can only lead to problems for you. You must be able to carry through on the image you create. You must be comfortable with it.

An interesting experiment was carried out some years ago that demonstrates the effect your image has on the way people respond to you. A tape was made by a doctor about some medical research. The tape was played for three different audiences, the members of each having been selected at random. The tape was introduced differently each time and questions were asked at the conclusion of the tape. One group was told that the presenter was a renowned medical researcher, another that he was a professional actor reading a script, and another that he was a tried and convicted medical quack. The audience who had been told that this was a medical researcher remembered the presentation very well when questioned on it, while the group that was told that they had the quack didn't remember the talk at all.   Those who were told they had the actor remembered some, but not all, of the presentation.

What Are Your Speech Patterns?

Professor Higgins of *My Fair Lady* demonstrated that a person's speech was the key to his or her position in society. This may have been more true in class-conscious England at the turn of the century than in the United States now, but I don't really think so. You will find that people are very aware of the speech of others and still classify people according to their speech patterns.

There are two things that must be considered here. One is what you say and the other is how you say it. Some people have a regional or a foreign accent. You may or may not want to change this. There is nothing wrong with having an accent but some accents are considered to be "lower class" or a sign of illiteracy. I will not try to define what that means. I just know that is the case. We are not talking about what is right, but about the image you are creating. If you want to be considered intelligent, you will have to sound intelligent. This is related to many things including tone of voice, accent, vocabulary and grammar. There is never any excuse for using poor grammar or incorrect vocabulary. Tape yourself and study your accent. Ask a friend who comes from another part of the country to listen to your accent on tape. What do they think about your accent? Is it charming and regional or does it appear ignorant? How can you change it just enough to be effective without losing your personal charm?

For some, there is the matter of tone or placement of voice. Listen to yourself on a tape recorder. Is your voice pleasing? Do you sound nasty and belligerent or friendly and intelligent? Would you like to listen to yourself? There are exercises you can do to develop a more pleasing voice. One factor in learning to create the new image is that your speech should be appropriate. Enrich it. Always be certain that you are

198

using words correctly. One way to improve your vocabulary is to read a great deal. Vary what you read. This will not only improve your vocabulary but also give you new things to think about and talk about. Don't let your conversation be nothing but a string of anecdotes.

What do you talk about? Do you monopolize the conversation? One way to make friends and influence people is to be a good listener. Try to remember details about the lives of people you have been introduced to previously. Is your conversation dominated by cliches and the recounting of old stories? Is this appropriate? For some situations, it is, while for other situations, it is not.

Try to develop a good internal barometer. Think about people who have the kind of position you want to have. What do they talk about? You can't talk about work all the time. You have to be able to carry on light conversation with your associates. This may mean learning about politics, sports, classical music, or the latest rock concert. Whatever you need to do in order to reach proficiency, learn to converse with your associates and those on the level you wish to reach.

199

If you have to make a presentation, tape it first and listen to a playback of it. What things can you correct? Practice it until you are comfortable with the presentation. You may want to have a friend listen to you on tape, help you analyze your voice and plan any changes you may need to make. Don't be insulted by what they tell you.

You, the Person

When one of my family is staring into space, we ask "are you in there?" Sometimes the person will answer yes and smile and sometimes there will be no answer because they are too far away in thought.

Who are you inside your body? What is it that no mirror can ever show? Do you know this part of yourself? How do others perceive you? Personality, psychology, and being are all words that might be used. When you say, "He or she doesn't understand me," what do you mean by the "me"? This is a complicated concept, but one you must understand because it is a very large part of the image.

Do you like yourself? Would you like to have yourself for a friend, for a fellow worker, or for a boss? What parts of you do you like best? What parts of you do you like least?

What would you like to change about your life? What would you like to change about yourself?

Exercise 17.4

Take another piece of paper out and make another list. If you had to change three things about yourself that are not part of appearance but are part of your personality, what would you change?

1 _____
2 _____
3 _____
4 _____
5 _____
6 _____
7 _____
8 _____
9 _____
10 _____

Are you too quiet and shy or are you too loud? Are you generally happy or unhappy? Are you a workaholic or are you lazy? Are you quick or are you slow? Do you make friends easily or only with difficulty? Take that paper and write down ten positive things about yourself. Take that same paper and in another column write down five negative things about yourself. How can you build on the positive and eliminate the negative aspects of your personality? If you can change the things you feel are negative, others will respond to you differently. Will you feel comfortable with these changes? Many of these characteristics may be important in your search for a new position. Today there is much emphasis on being a team player. Don't pretend to be one if that is not your style.

Consider why it is not your style. What is your style? Are you aggressive enough? Are you too aggressive? Would your current level of aggressiveness be a plus or a minus in your new position? Remember you should be planning for the new career you want, rather than your present situation.

Will "the real you" be happy in the new position? Think about the characteristics you are most happy about. Will these fit in with the characteristics that are needed in your newly chosen career? Changing isn't what's really important. You must change to the right thing.

What values are important to you? You will generally not want to change your value system. Will your old values fit with your new position? Does the image you create fit in with your new value system?

If you are going to create a new image, that image must be able to stand the test of time. It cannot only be a matter of appearance and a few well-chosen grammatical phrases. It must go to the heart of your personality. Do others see you as you see yourself? Will others perceive your new image of you? Will it be so different that your old friends and family will not understand it?

201

You have to remember that others may not be part of the creation of your new image nor may they really want you to change. You must be ready for possible rejection of the new image on the part of those who thought they loved the "old you". You must be responsive to this situation. You may have a number of difficulties to overcome. If you are not happy with "the old you" it may be necessary for you to change. You must explain this to those who are close to you. It will not always be easy and you must be prepared to explain and defend your new self.

In order to do this you must understand your personality. If you were a naturally shy person and suddenly become very open and talkative, it would be noticed. The reverse is also true. What characteristics of the new image are very important to you? What you are trying to accomplish? How can you make this clear to those who are close to you? None of us exists in isolation. It is important to remember that.

What image do you present as a worker? What skills are apparent to the person who might be considering hiring you? What impression do you make on an interviewer? Which sides of your personality are most apparent in an interview? Is this the "real" you? Are you trying to project something that is not true?

Analyze your image and decide what elements must be changed to create the image you want to project.

Develop a step-by-step program for creating a new image. It will have components that relate to your physical characteristics, your appearance, your speech, your work habits and your ideas.

202

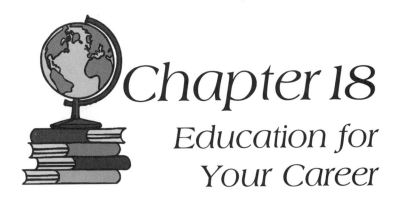

Chapter 18
Education for Your Career

Obtaining the Necessary Skills

Wanting a new position or career is not enough. In order to obtain that first job on the career ladder, you will have to demonstrate you have the skills required for the new position. In many cases this can be accomplished only through formal education, which is a major stumbling block for many people. In some cases, people who have just finished a college degree (with all of its costs) now find they don't like the career for which they have been preparing. Others did not pursue an education that would lead to a career and now find that they must go back to school. Still others are hopelessly out of date in one area and might as well consider entering a new career instead of re-training for the old one. Faced with the necessity of returning to school, some individuals foolishly abandon their new goal, rather than obtain the needed training.

Returning to school is not easy. In many cases, however, it is an absolute necessity. When you are changing careers, you are at a disadvantage without the right education.

- You may not have the skills necessary to carry out the position.
- You may not know you do not have the skills or even what the needed skills are.
- You may not have a method for documenting that you do indeed have the necessary skills for the position.

The employer who hires a young person straight out of school has a record and academic references to use as part of the hiring assessment.

This individual has current knowledge in the field in which he/she is being hired. Both the employer and the employee make some assumptions that the proper preparation for the position has occurred. They place some security in the academic program that prepared and certified the student. Although many may refer to a degree as just a piece of paper, it is far more than that in today's marketplace. Whether the training is relevant or not by your standard, it is a license today for performing many jobs.

The person who is involved in a career change brings a different set of credentials, which in many cases look a little bit like Swiss cheese. There is some substance which is of high quality, but there are also a lot of holes.

The role of an academic institution, whether it be a college or some form of vocational school, is more complex than the potential student sometimes understand.

"The school teaches me what I need to know," you say. "It gives me a degree." This phrase is absolutely true, but it implies much more than you may realize.

If you are planning to make a career change, there are a number of questions you will have to answer.

- Do I need additional formal training in a college or university?
- Do I need to have a specific degree?
- Do I need to take a training program or a program which will give me preparation to take a licensing exam?
- What kind of training do I need?
- What is the best place I can go to get that training?
- What do I have to do to prepare myself and my family for the emotional reality of my going back to school?
- What skills will I need if I am returning to school?
- Are there training programs or courses which will serve my needs rather than going back to a college based program?
- What will it cost me to get the training?
- Where will I find the money?

204

Although some discussion of these questions is presented in this chapter, the reader who wants a more extensive preparation on these topics should refer to books such as my first book to be published which is titled *Are You Ready?: A Survival Manual for Women Returning to School*. Although the title implies that the book is for women, much of the material included is quite valid for men as well. I also have a new book that I am currently writing which has the working title How to Survive Returning to School. You may find the older book in the library as it is not still available in bookstores.

Do You Need Additional Formal Training?

There are certain authors who have written about career change who either imply or state directly that you do not need formal training for a career change. These statements may be encouraging to some who want to plunge into their newly selected area, but I cannot help believe that this is false encouragement. In most cases, although indeed not in all, preparation in the new area is certainly needed. Let us think about some possible examples, which are related to magazine articles you may have read on the subject.

205

You have been doing volunteer work, organizing individuals and collecting a substantial amount of money for charity. You are now able to put this on your resume as a qualification and are prepared to enter the world of business as a manager. It is true that this accomplishment will help fill out your resume, but it will never replace "real" work experience as a paid manager of a business and/or an MBA. You may say this experience gave you far more opportunity and responsibility than you would ever have had in a work position. That may be the case. Right and reason, however, have not yet replaced reality. The person who has been in the work force in a job directly related to the one being sought will have a distinct advantage over the person who has not held such a position. The person who has just finished an educational program directly related to the position being sought also has an advantage. His or her skills are hopefully up to date.

You often hear the complaint, particularly among young people, "I can't get a job without experience and I can't get the experience." That may be an unfortunate truth but you can arrange to reinforce your academic preparation, at the very least.

While it is true you may not need to attend college or get an advanced degree to qualify for certain positions, you are severely limiting yourself in potential development of that career for you. There are very few careers in which you can advance without a college or technical degree. Even careers such as art, music and the theater which were formerly less demanding of degrees than performance are slowly shifting over as excellent educational programs have been developed. While programs which specialize in computers have proliferated in colleges and universities in the last twenty years, the changes in the field occur so fast that many university programs are not able to operate at the cutting edge. Some people will say that they are not getting as much from their college program as they might from a specialized course. While this is true in many cases, you will find that the employers often hire the university trained person over the one without a degree for a number of reasons. One is that having the University degree shows a capacity for learning new material which will be required over the length of time during which the employee works for the company. The new hire can always be sent to a technical course to pick up necessary information in an area which is required by the company. In recent years very advanced (and expensive) courses have been developed by certain companies which establish credentials for the students in certain computer areas. These courses are invaluable for updating or advancing the knowledge of participants who may have had prior training in the areas of computers. Unless you have extensive knowledge about computers already, these courses would be much too difficult. If, however, you have a great deal of practical experience, but little formal training, they may provide you with the training you need to hold intermediate level jobs.

Many individuals have chosen to attend a technical school or vocational school and found that they were well prepared for the starting position in their chosen field. They often also find, howev-

206

er, that they can't get promoted to higher level positions. Experience is a good teacher, but she is no substitute for credentials. With credentials you can get experience. Without credentials, you may only get lower level experience and lower level employment.

There are some areas in which you can demonstrate your ability without necessarily going to school, although, as stated above, this is rapidly changing. If you are seeking a career in an area which demands creative skills, you will have to prepare a portfolio. This will include samples of your work-photography, writing, layouts, designs, computer programs, art work or whatever else which may fall into related areas of creative arts. In the areas of crafts, music or films, it might be necessary to provide a technical portfolio with video tapes recording examples of your work.

It is possible to maintain and even develop further skills in creative areas without attending formal classes. In some cases, formal academic training inhibits creativity, while in others it can advance knowledge and technique. If you are going to use the portfolio route rather than documentation of recent formal education be certain that your portfolio looks professional. It should follow the format which graduates of a formal university program are instructed to follow. You could check with a recent graduate of a formal program or with an instructor in the program. Some of them may be interested in helping you a little, even though you are not able to enter their program, if they feel you have talent and you broach the question in the correct manner.

207

Many people feel that because they can do something they are able to teach it. This is often not true. Teaching is a skill in itself. Knowledge of a field is not all you need. You will need some training in the method of teaching your subject as well as in interpersonal relations with your students. In particular, you may have to meet specific requirements in order to teach. These requirements differ according to geographic location, grade level and the subject matter involved. Your local school board and/or department of education at a local college can tell you how to find out about the requirements which would apply to you. Even if courses in teaching are not required, you may be well advised to take them.

Are you up-to-date in the field of your choice? This is the key question. What does a recent graduate know about the field you have chosen? You can find this out by taking a look at the courses that are offered and at the books used for those courses. They can be found in college bookstores. Do you know most of the material? Are you comfortable with it? Can you use all the jargon of the field? Do you even know what the latest terms are? Are you comfortable with them? If the answer is an unqualified "yes" then you may not need any additional education, but do not fool yourself on this crucial question. You may be able to fool your future employer long enough to get the job, but how will you perform? Could you do the job? Could you keep the job?

Are your skills up to an appropriate performance standard? This may include operating a specific piece of equipment. There have been many changes in certain equipment. Sometimes it appears that the computer is taking over the world, word processing has revolutionized many areas and typewriters are kept in a closet for use in filling out forms that are not on the computer. Scanners are now being used to put complex forms on the computer..

Are you limiting your opportunities by depending on outdated skills and knowledge? Could you open up brand new areas for yourself if you did go back to school? Are you eliminating something from your list of possibilities because of the fact that you would have to go back to school to accomplish it?

If you are satisfied that with your knowledge and skill level, you may not need to go back to school. Make that decision with full knowledge of yourself and your opportunities, however.   If you do decide to take a course or a program, you should begin your decision_making process with the question of the right curriculum and then select the school that will give you that curriculum.

The Curriculum

Although accrediting bodies and professional organizations have some input, you must remember that the schools design curricula. Different courses are chosen, majors developed and a degree given by a particular institution. The institution may

use guidelines provided by accrediting agencies or state departments of education or professional associations, but it still has great freedom. Curricula at two different institutions may be quite similar but this is not always the case. Curriculum at one institution may appear to be very current and at another it may not have changed essentially in twenty years even though course titles are the same. This is true of colleges and universities, as well as professional and vocational schools. Not all degrees lead to a career. This is an important thing to remember. This is not the fault of the institution, nor a flaw in the program. Many students have followed a particular major only to discover that they could not get a job using their knowledge when they graduated. Remember that there are reasons for choosing a particular major other than preparing for a career, but careers are the focus of this book.

The university has a responsibility to provide education and maintain knowledge about areas of scholarship which are somewhat unique and not necessarily job-related. There are many courses of study that are important in themselves but may not be job related. It is for you to determine if a particular course of study will lead to the career you want. Just getting a college degree, for example, will not open up all doors for you, although it will open some.

Curricula at different schools are different. Some people believe that if you are taking the same major at two different schools you will have basically the same program. This is not generally true. Study and compare curricula for the same program title. Are the requirements the same?

If you find that you went to the wrong school or if you find you took the wrong program, you may try to blame, in part, the counseling service of the institution. You must really look to yourself. You have to be responsible for planning your college program. You will have to be aggressive in asking questions and making comparisons. This move is yours.

Certification and Accreditation

One role that a learning institution plays is as a certifying body. The university certifies that you have certain knowledge

209

in specific areas. The credibility of the university reflects on you. If the institution you attended has a very good reputation, you will generally be a more desirable job candidate. Never let anyone tell you that "It doesn't matter where you graduated from as long as you have a college degree." That is far from true.

An important element is the accreditation of the institution itself. All institutions are not of the same quality. In order to monitor the performance of schools and universities, accrediting agencies have been formed. Dividing the country into regions, these accrediting agencies work together and exchange information. Schools in one region will accept the accreditation of an institution made by the agency in their own region or by one of the other regional accrediting agencies. If you are going to attend a college, be certain that it has been ACCREDITED by one of the REGIONAL accrediting agencies. Some schools that are not accredited try to tell you that accreditation doesn't matter. It does. Credits obtained at a college that is not accredited generally will not be accepted by an accredited school if you transfer. They may not be accepted by state licensing agencies either. Quality varies even among accredited schools. Be cautious, you are dealing with your future.

If you want to check on an institution, call or write to the accrediting agency for your region. You can probably get the name of the executive director from your library. The six major accrediting agencies and the states they represent are:

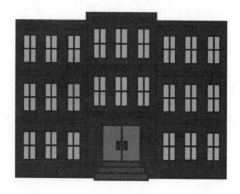

Middle States Association of Colleges and Secondary Schools:

3624 Market Street

Philadelphia, Pa 19104

(215) 662-5603

includes: Delaware, District of Columbia, Maryland, New Jersey, New York, Pennsylvania, Canal Zone, Puerto Rico, Virgin Islands.

New England Association of Schools and Colleges

209 Burlington Road

Bedford, Mass 01730

(781) 271-0022 FAX (617) 271-0950

includes: Connecticut, Maine, Massachusetts, New Hampshire, Rhode Island, Vermont.

North Central Association of Colleges and Secondary schools

Arizona State University

Box 873011

Tempe, AZ 85287-3011

(800) 621-7440 or (312) 263-0456

includes: Arizona, Arkansas, Colorado, Illinois, Indiana, Iow, Kansas, Michigan, Minnesota, Missouri, Nebraska, New Mexico, North Dakota, Ohio, Oklahoma, South Dakota, West Virginia, Wisconsin, Wyoming.

Northwest Association of Secondary and Higher Schools:

1910 University Drive

Boise, ID 83725-1060

includes: Alaska, Idaho, Montana, Nevada, Oregon, Utah, Viginia, Washington.

(208)426-5727

Southern Association of Colleges and Schools

1866 Southern Lane

Decatur Georgia 30033-4097

(404) 679-4500 (800) 248-7701

includes: Alabama, Florida, Georgia, Kentucky, Louisiana, Mississippi, North Carolina, South Carolina, Tennessee, Texas, Virginia.

Western Association of Colleges and Schools

533 Airport Blvd Suite 200

Burlingame, California 94010

(650)696-1060

includes: California and Hawaii

211

While these have been the correct addresses and phone numbers for these agencies for years, please check them before you call or write. The telephone companies have been changing numbers recently, particularly with regard to area codes and new numbers become scarce.

Don't assume things. Find out if a school and program you are considering are properly accredited before you enter the institution.

In addition to verifying the accreditation of the institution, you should determine if the specific career for which you are preparing requires a license or a special accreditation on the part of the program. Will the program you are entering qualify you to sit for licensing exams? In some cases programs may be applying for this specialized accreditation. Identify the program status and its significance. For example, courses to be used to obtain a teaching license must be approved by the Department of Education of the state in which you are seeking to be licensed not the state in which the college is located. You should check with the state in which you will be teaching to find out what you must do to get a teaching license there. Many professional programs such as law and medicine must be approved by professional associations. Check with the appropriate professional association to determine if a program you are considering has the necessary approval.

Selecting the Correct Program

If you have already selected a new career, your problems in selecting a specific program will be somewhat reduced. If there is more than one accredited institution in your area, compare the programs carefully. You may not want to enter a college program. Think this out carefully. A vocational program may appear to be the appropriate one for you. How do employers react to someone applying for the desired position who does not have a college degree and/or experience in the field? Remember, a person changing careers or returning to work will be viewed differently from a young person starting out. If you already have a degree you have credentials. This is important. If you do not have a degree, you may want to consider the extra time needed to get a degree as a good investment. Many students who have completed a technical program and decided later that they wanted a college degree have found that their work in a non-accredited technical or vocational school will not be accepted for transfer to a college program. The time and money they have spent are wasted in terms of college credit. Determine all of these factors before you make your final program selection.

Remember not all courses offered by a university are for college credit or will count towards a degree. Not all courses offered by one program in a university are accepted for transfer credit in another program at the same university or to a similar program at another university. Some universities will only transfer a limited number of courses even if you did well at the other institution. Some times courses get too "old" and will not be accepted for credit towards requirements for a degree in a specific major even at the same university. This is a reasonable academic rule but has come as a terrible surprise to many students.

213

Another important thing to investigate is the level of position you can obtain in the field of your choice with the degree you are seeking. For example, there are not very many positions for bachelor's degree graduates in psychology or in physics. Most positions in these areas require advanced training. There are, however, high level positions for those with bachelor's degrees in engineering, computer science and business. This situation may change, of course, but the change would be in the direction of a greater emphasis on education. Be sure to determine exactly what you need to get the position you are seeking.

The Admission Process

After you have selected the school and the program, you will have to consider what you must do to gain admittance to the program. Admission requirements vary according to the institution and sometimes within programs in the same institutions.

Some universities require that you submit scores from the College Board Entrance Exams or Standard Aptitude Tests, (SAT's). These are given several times a year at specific loca-  tions. You cannot just show up at one of the exam centers. You must make a reservation by a specific date. The guidance office at a nearby high school or college can give you information concerning this exam, or you can write directly to The College Board 888 Seventh Avenue, New York, New York, 10019. If you desire to enter a college or university which requires this exam you will have to make your preparations many months in advance. You will see a requirement for S.A.T. scores on some application forms. These are the same thing.

When you register for this exam, you will get a little booklet containing some sample questions and answers. These seem simple but don't let them fool you. The questions in the booklet are only samples of the types of questions you will be asked. The actual questions will be much harder. Find some high school students who are preparing for the college boards and they will explain to you just how difficult these tests are. The score you get on these exams will often determine which schools you are admitted to. You may not have taken this type of exam for a while.. Study for it. I can not say this too strongly. The people who make up the exam say you can't study for it, but that is not true.

Purchase one or more of the books that are written to help you take these exams. They are available at most bookstores and can be special ordered for you by other bookstores or by on-line sources. They are often found in the bookstores of colleges. These books contain sample questions and sample tests. The test includes a verbal part and a mathematical part, both of which include questions regarding "thinking skills". In addition, there are specialized subject matter tests. You may not need to take the specialized tests. Check with the school to which you are applying. Take the standard tests and time yourself. You may be able to answer the questions but it may take you too much time. You are given a limited amount of time to answer each part of the test. The practice books will specify the amount of time for each test section. The score you get on this exam may determine whether or not you will get into the college and program of your choice. Optimize your opportunity to do well.

In addition to the books, there are software programs which will test you on these type of tests as well and are excellent for enhancing your time in answering the questions.

Some institutions have open admissions policies. This means that you will not have to take an entrance exam. It does not mean that you can do poorly in your work once you have entered the institution. If you have an admission interview, be open about your reasons for attending the school. This is especially true if you are a returning student. Your motivation may be an important factor in the decision about whether to admit you. Although some schools do not have waiting lists, others do. Do not give up if you are rejected at one institution. Waiting lists are very valid instruments. Just because you see articles about the buyers market for students, do not think this is the case at all colleges. If you are rejected by a number of different institutions, ask those schools why you were turned down. This is very important information. Make use of it to prepare yourself for another try at getting admitted.

215

Learning Styles

If you do get in, will you be able to do the work? This is a question which many students ask themselves. The answer sometimes prompts students to drop out before they even start. There are many elements involved when one is returning to school. There is the family situation, the question of time management, the survival under stress and there is the sharpening of basic skills.

In Are You Ready? I devoted a number of pages to the elements that are involved in your making the decision to return to school, and to steps that will help you and your family make the adjustment. I will not cover those elements here, but it is appropriate to speak about stress. Stress is a prominent component of present day living. In an earlier chapter, a table was presented that indicated a value for various stress elements in our lives. Changing careers is definitely stressful. If you have to add the element of returning to school to this, you will increase your stress.

In order to minimize this component, you must take every opportunity to make things easier for yourself. This includes visiting the campus in advance of your first class in order to identify the location of all the places you need to find on your first couple of days. It very definitely includes improving your skills in a number of areas. You will have to learn how to read for information, how to write a term paper, how to take tests, how to use the library and above all how to use a computer to research and write your papers.

Going to college involves interaction with fellow students. If you are substantially older than the other students in your classes you will have to develop a technique for interacting with them. Do not assume that you will be older than all of your fellow students or that because you are older, you will not fit into your classes. The average age at academic institutions has been creeping upward over the last twenty years. The local state institution in my community quotes twenty-eight years as their average age. Since I know they serve a number of eighteen to twenty-two year olds this means that they must have a large number of students at the other end of the scale as well to push up the average. The admissions office at schools in which you are interested can give you this information. Times are changing rapidly and you may be surprised when you see the makeup of the classes you are attending.

A basic element in your success in college will be your preparation in the basic skills. Mathematics will be important for certain programs and these skills must be at your fingertips. Confidence is imperative here. Computers are used in many classes in which they are relevant.

Be certain that you can see the computer screen well. Your vision may be sufficient to do your present tasks but the increased reading and computer work may demand better sight. Have you vision tested before you begin your classes.

The most important factor will be your ability to

216

communicate. Your ability to read, write and speak effectively will determine not only your success in your academic program but your fate in your new field. You may also need to increase your rate of reading. The material you will be reading is far different from reading the daily newspaper or a favorite magazine. It does not count as "reading" unless you understand what you are reading. There are few areas in which communication is not a vital ingredient but these areas generally depend on the degree of development of another skill. You may want to be a fine dancer, mechanic, or artist. You may or may not need to develop what is generally termed communication for your particular field, but you will need it if you are to be successful as a person. Most colleges, particularly those which offer a two year degree, have centers which will assess your basic skills and non-credit courses to improve them. Some also have courses in writing term papers and centers that will help you with this area of college requirements. It is not only the returning student who may need help here. Many students just out of high school have difficulty with basic skills and writing papers.

217

Perhaps the most important element for you in preparing to enter a college program is to become comfortable using a computer. There are many who will say "I am too old to learn computers" or "I'd never understand how a computer works." Remember that you probably drive a car all of the time and don't know how the car works. Using a computer does not mean that you have to understand how it works either. The first thing you need to learn is how to use a word processing program. Some schools have selected a particular word processing program and have installed that program on the computers which they have available for student use. Don't get a program which is too simple. While it may seem a good choice to you when you are first learning to use it, you will soon outgrow it. It may also not be compatible with programs used by your classmates and the college itself. Microsoft Word and Corel's Word perfect are two excellent programs which are currently on the market. Some high school evening programs give inexpensive classes in using a computer and using one of these word processing programs. Learn a major program, not a simplified version. Don't start college without being prepared in these areas.

Finding Money for School

I can't afford to go back to school, you might be saying.
The problem of paying for college and other professional
training is a severe one but there are a number of loan and
grant programs on the federal, state, and community level
which will help you. Many schools offer aid specifically
designed for the returning student. The topic of finding
money for college is so extensive that my husband, Robert L. Burke and I have written a series of books on College Money including *College Money in Florida, College
Money in New England*, and *College Money in New York/New Jersey*. These books
will give you information you need to find the funding for your educational program.
And don't forget all of that information on the Internet.

The Internship

218

If you are still in college or graduate school, the best way to gain the experience
and the money you need is to obtain an internship. Many businesses make an
arrangement with an institution to provide an opportunity for a student to gain
hands on experience while still under the supervision of the college. This is an effort
on the part of the industry to develop applicants for their industry who will not just
be novices at graduation.

They will have the high level of theory needed to do the job, but they will also have
the practical experience needed to actually do the job.

How is this different, you may ask, from getting a part-time job in the same field
on your own? There are several differences. First of all, the program is integrated with
your college courses and you may get college credit for the work done which will
move you along toward graduation. The tasks you will do in the course of the internship may be at a higher level than you would be assigned as a part-time employee.
You will be under the supervision of one or more individuals at the place of employment who will show you what to do and answer your questions. Generally these

supervisors are high level employees of the company. You will also be under the supervision of a college coordinator who may be a professor who can answer questions about the tasks you are performing as well. You will gain experience at a much higher level than you could have as an entry level employee.

As you will be an intern, and therefore only at the place of work for a set period of time such as six weeks or a term, the usual jealousies between old employees and new employees will not develop. You will find that people who would normally be your competitors as a new employee with be pleased to show you their way of doing things which may indeed be superior to what the book says to do.

Salaries for internships vary. Some internships provide no salary and you have to pay your tuition for credit for the course. Others give a modest salary while still others provide a payment comparable to what a regular employee would receive in that field.

There are colleges whose total programs are based on an internship program. Their engineers take longer than four years to complete their degree because they alternate various numbers of school semesters with work semesters. The money earned during the work semesters helps to support them during the school semesters. Often interns are asked to come back for several interning sessions at the same company, being almost assured of a job when they graduate.

The advantages to the companies are clear. They get an opportunity to try out graduates from a particular institution before they hire them. This has proved to be very beneficial to new programs at institutions. Some new graduate programs such as law schools have had difficulty in placing their graduates in the first few years of their existence. Employers want to take graduates from schools with which they have had previous experience but they often are willing to give an internship opportunity to students from new programs. In the process, they are made aware of the abilities of these students, especially students who have returned to school, and so the process is good for the institution as well as for the students and the employers.

In addition to actual work, skills interns learn the customs, courtesies, and dress required by the job in their proposed field before making the final commitment. If you have the opportunity to take an internship, don't hesitate to do so.

Meeting the New Demands

Returning to school will make many demands on you. You must realize this. You will have to be prepared to modify your life, to devote the needed time to your family, your work and your school work. This is not a trivial problem.

Returning to school is not a casual thing. It must be planned. For some, this planning must be done well in advance of the starting date of classes; it should begin by developing the basic skills. It is not unusual to be afraid when thinking about returning to school. The fear of failure can keep you from even starting. Think 220 about all the things you must do to prepare for college and do the preparation.

1. Pick the right program in the right college.
2. Learn your way around the school and make friends with your fellow students.
3. Improve your communication skills.
4. Learn to write papers since many of your grades will depend on your ability to produce research papers.
5. Learn to use a computer and the word processing program that is available at your chosen school. Although it is very useful to have a computer of your own, many schools also provide computers for student use.
6. Learn to use a computer before you buy one, if possible, so that you can better choose one that will meet your needs. Some institutions are now requiring their students to have laptop computers that can be brought to class and are installing the necessary plugs in libraries for student computer use.
7. Plan a time schedule that will allow you to get your academic work finished on time and yet leave a piece of your life for your family and for living in general.
8. Organizing time is an essential part of your preparation for a career.

Chapter 19
Communication
Skills

The Three "R's"

Remember the three "R's"? Reading, writing, and 'rithmetic are three skills that you will obviously need if you are going to undertake any kind of educational program. You realize this, I am certain. You may tell me your math is a little rusty but of course you can read and write. You learned these skills in grammar school just like everyone else. You use them every day. You read the paper in the morning and perhaps a novel occasionally. You leave notes for your husband or wife and the kids. Perhaps you even write a letter to your parents and to Aunt Tilly once in a while except that the telephone is so much handier and that has been replaced now by the use of e-mail. If you are a younger student you may tell me that you just got out of high school or college last June or a few years ago. Obviously you can read and write.

Please take a good look at your ability to read and write. College will make very strenuous demands on these abilities. Some high schools will focus on "answers" and give many multiple choice exams. They certainly are easier to grade. Some places have provisions for these exams to be graded by machine. And they certainly eliminate some of the controversy as to whether a essay answer is "correct" and worth a certain number of points. In many colleges you will get extensive reading assignments and have to prepare research papers which will involve both reading and writing. When the term "reading" is used here it refers to reading for content and reading for understanding, not just being able to recognize the words.

The fact is not everyone learned to read and write well and some people cannot read on a level which is needed for them to perform successfully in college or other specialized schools.

As meritorious as all your reading and writing may be, they do not completely prepare you for entering those hallowed halls of college or graduate school.

Arming yourself with the right tools for school is not the only reason to improve your communication skills. Many positions in industry require that you comprehend complex material, and employers complain they are faced with potential employees who cannot even fill out employment applications. Individuals who are changing careers often find they must obtain some additional education or training before they can secure their position. This may be in a college, a vocational school or in a training program in a company. In all cases it will demand a high level of reading proficiency. Actually doing the job may also require reading skills even if it is a job that involves "things". There is a sad tale about a navy ship that sank because one of the sailors could not read the instructions which were written on a particular piece of equipment . Doing the task wrong set up a series of events that finally caused the ship to sink. I do not know how many lives were lost because of that man's inability to truly understand what he read.

Reading for College Success

Reading in college and graduate school is marked by the volume of material you have to digest, the level on which it is written, and the amount of information you have to obtain from the printed page. I am not trying to frighten you, but even those who are omnivorous readers of light material find they have problems when they try to keep up with their college and graduate school assignments. A friend of mine, who, like me, reads every piece of print in sight, including the cereal box on the breakfast table, found herself pressed when she went back to get her Master's degree in library science. She discovered she had to give up her light reading during that period. Light reading and heavy reading are such different techniques that she found that she could not get involved with both at the same time. Even if you are a good reader, you may find that the same is true.

Before you can improve your reading ability you have to assess just where you are. There are many components to reading that must be evaluated separately. A number of tests are designed to do this and many are related to a certain grade level in school. There are programs all over the country, some private and some public, which can help you assess and remediate your reading ability. You may find these programs in the same place as you found the vocational testing programs which were previously discussed. Adult programs in high schools, vocational schools and community colleges often offer reading evaluation tests to individuals even if they are not yet enrolled in the institution's programs. The U.S. government and state governments often fund such programs on the local level. Check with your local high school guidance office for information.

223

Colleges have introduced remedial reading programs to help incoming students. Open admission policies in some schools allow students to enter on the basis of having graduated from high school, but shocking results have been produced on some of the reading assessment tests. A frightening percentage of incoming freshmen read on the third to sixth grade level. Do you think that you might fall into that group? Even if you are not in that position you might find that you do not test as well as you think you will.

Before you enter testing and re-mediation programs, let us do some self-assessment. The reading components that we will discuss are comprehension, vocabulary, speed, and timing.

Reading Comprehension

1. Comprehension is the most important of these components for the college student. The word itself means understanding, and reading without understanding is a useless task. It doesn't matter how fast you read if you don't understand what you are reading. It is a little bit like the story about the driver who had taken the wrong road. He said he was lost but he was making great time.

To have good comprehension you must understand not only the meaning of the individual words, but also the meaning of the words when they are used together. There may be implications, as well as information, that must be gained from a phrase or paragraph. You will not only have to improve your understanding of words but your understanding of words grouped together. This is a case where the whole is often greater than the sum of the parts.

224 How can you evaluate your ability to comprehend material? First of all, you must identify the kinds of material you will be using in the program you will enter. You can do this by getting the titles of the books you would be using from the college bookstore or the department of study in the institution. If you do not want to buy books in advance, you can then check out the same or similar books from the library. If you do want to buy some, but the books are not yet available in the bookstore, you may be able to order them over the Internet from Amazon.com, Borders or Barnes and Noble.

Read a section of the book and try to do some of the following things.

1. Find a title for the section you have just read. This should indicate the point of the material.
2. Write a topic sentence which summarizes the material.
3. Take each paragraph on a page and try to summarize it in a single sentence.
4. If you are having difficulty doing this, try rephrasing the sentences in a single paragraph on a sentence-by-sentence basis. If you can rephrase material you probably understand it. If you cannot, you probably are unsure of it.
5. Make a list of the factual items included in the material.

6. Make a list of any words you are not able to define. I don't mean you just recognize the word but that you could construct a definition which you could give to a friend who didn't know what the word meant and they would understand its meaning from what you said. We often have sketchy concepts about certain words without really understanding their true meaning.

7. If you are able to get a book that has questions at the end of the chapter, try to read a section and without looking up the material, answer the questions.

How do you know if you have done well? For the factual information you can check the answers with the material in the text. The evaluation of the summary, title and topic sentence will require the assistance of someone who has been successful in similar courses. You can, with practice, gain confidence as you learn, but you may need some initial help.

Retention is another component which is closely related to comprehension. Comprehension measures what you understand. Retention measures how long you remember what you have read or studied.

You may be interested in getting an idea of your grade level for comprehension, To get an approximate idea of your reading level, obtain some textbooks which give some indication of the grade level. If you have children in school, you may be able to use some of their books or one of their teachers may help you obtain some for the grade level you desire. The school librarian or the principal may also help you if you explain your plan. In larger school systems there is generally a library for teachers to obtain materials. You might try there. You will probably have to use the books in the library. Some libraries also have books which are graded according to the reading level. The children's librarian may be of help to you.

Find the books with the reading level with which you are really comfortable. These may be high school textbooks written on a twelfth grade level or they may be far below that level. This will give you a rough approximation of your reading level. Sometimes this is not indicated in the book itself, but the teacher who loans you the book would be able to tell you the grade level for which it was written. It is often not the grade level in which it is used. Many schools must teach at below grade level in

225

some classes while in other classes it is done at above grade level. Grade level will be indicated in the teacher's manual he or she received with the book. Remember, just because the book is used on the eighth grade level, for example, does not mean it is written on an eighth grade reading level. It may be far below that level. A far better technique would be to take a test using one of the standard reading tests. There are a number which have been designed for use by adults. You may be able to arrange to take such a test through a local community college or adult education program at a vocational school.

Improving Your Vocabulary

All of us have a number of different vocabularies. For example, there is our speaking vocabulary, our reading vocabulary and our writing vocabulary. We use different words depending on our subject matter and the context. We use a different vocabulary when speaking to a small child than we would use in writing a formal report.

226   If you work to increase your reading recognition vocabulary you will also be increasing your written vocabulary. Make an investment in a pocket dictionary; carry it with you and read it. You can learn a new word while you are waiting for the light to change or for a line to move. Keep a list of your new words and keep going over them. Don't forget to use them. As a word becomes part of both your reading and writing vocabulary, you can remove it from your working list.

Every subject matter has its own vocabulary, its own jargon. Be certain you know the jargon of the subject you are going to study. Again, you can get a college level textbook in the subject matter. This time, go to the index in the back of the book. Be certain that you know the meaning of every word in the index. To "know'" the meaning means you can write a definition in your own words, not that you sort of remember hearing the word used at some

time, and that you can use it. Look up new words and add them to your vocabulary list. As they become part of your vocabulary, you again can remove them from the list.

Increasing Your Reading Speed

You may have seen ads for increasing your reading speed although they are not as frequent as they once were. Remember that while comprehension is more important than speed, you cannot neglect the question of how fast you read. You will have a substantial amount of material to read and only a limited amount of time. If you can increase your reading speed, with full comprehension, you will have effectively increased the number of hours in your day.

Your rate of reading will be related to the difficulty of the material. You will read a textbook much more slowly than a Reader's Digest article. Try a test to find out how fast you can read "ordinary" material. To do this you need a watch with an alarm or a friend who will watch the clock for you. Take a magazine article with average vocabulary. Count the number of words on five lines and divide your answer by five. You will then have an average value for the number of words per line. Have someone time you for sixty seconds while you read at your regular reading speed. You will then have to count the number of lines you have read during this minute. Multiply the number of lines by the average number of words per line and you will have the number of words read in a minute. How do you know the meaning of your rate (your wpm is the number of words you read per minute)? Are you fast or are you slow?

There are some general parameters which vary according to reading program but the ones I use for light reading are:

200 wpm or below	poor
300 wpm	average
400 wpm	good
over 500	excellent

227

The numbers above are not infallible. If you come out high on the scale, you can assume you are reading light material at a good rate. You can always increase that rate, however. If you come out with a poor score, you should definitely include a reading improvement program in your future. Now that you have your speed calculated for light reading, try the same thing with textbook material. Your rate will be lower than for light reading but working on comprehension and vocabulary should increase this if you have used good techniques to increase your light reading skill and eliminate bad habits. If you cannot take an "official" program, there are several things you can do to improve your reading speed.

Practicing your reading will serve to improve your speed. One of the first things you have to do is to find out what is slowing you down. Knowing how to read each word is only a part of reading. You also have to learn to put the words together. This puts us into the question of timing.

If you read one word at a time, you will not only be slow, you will also be reducing your comprehension. In order to make gains in both areas, you will have to learn to first read a couple of words at a time and then whole phrases.

A rather obvious, but sometimes neglected, solution is to have your eyes examined. Eyesight that was adequate for daily living may not be sharp enough for all the reading you will be doing.

Another problem that people have is one of letting the eyes go back over the words that have just been read. The eyes and then the mind are reading and rereading. It is as is as if you were going over going over the same thing same thing over and over over over. Think of how much extra time it would take you to read a page if you read like that and how it reduces your comprehension of the material. You might not do quite as much over-reading as shown above but most people are not aware of just how much they really do.

If you read a story out loud you know that it takes you much longer than if you read it to yourself. Some people unconsciously move their lips when they are reading and this slows them down. The movement may be very subtle. To determine if you have this habit, put your finger near your mouth when you are reading and see

228

if you can detect any movement. If you find that you are guilty of this, practice reading with your finger on your lips until you rid yourself of this habit.

If you find that you are an average reader and wish to increase your rate, try pacing yourself.   Set a task, in this case a number of words per minute, that is a little bit larger than your normal amount. Try and read a little more than you would read, on the average, in a five-minute period. Do this until you are comfortable and you will be reading at a your new rate. You should maintain the same level of comprehension at this new rate. You will gradually raise your reading speed, but do not fool yourself. You are not reading faster if you are understanding less because you are not really reading, you are just looking at words. There are many books written to improve your reading. My book, *Are You Ready? A Survival Manual for Women Returning to School,* has a more extensive section than has been presented here. If you are seriously interested in improving your reading, purchase or get a library copy of one of the many books that have been written specifically to improve your reading skills. The time you spend on improving your reading ability will be returned to you over and over again. If you had been a "non-reader" before, you may even find that you now enjoy reading.

229

Improving Your Writing Skills

One of the main activities of college students is writing papers. Graduate students are even more involved in this activity. Desperate, panic in their eyes, they will answer your inquiry into their state of desperation with, "I have to do a paper."

This is something new to many adults. When they went to high school they did not learn to write papers. But times have changed. My children started their first research paper in the fifth grade, complete with bibliography. This made life easier for them when they got to college. College professors complain that young people, who should have learned it in high school, still don't know how to write a paper. In any case, it is a task that will become very familiar before you graduate from college. Vocational programs do not usually require as many papers as college programs, but improving your skill in writing will still improve your success as a job applicant in many areas.

There are several steps you must follow when doing a paper.

- choose a topic
- establish a timetable
- obtain and use research materials
- record and make notes on the material
- find a pivotal point of view
- write the paper
- prepare the footnotes and the bibliography
- type the paper, preferably on a computer yourself but otherwise pay to have it typed. Most professors will not accept a paper that is not typed. It must also be clean, neat and free of typing errors and erasures. Corrections for misspellings are simple on the computer. Gone are the days when something has to be typed over and over.
- submit the paper on time

230 You may have a topic specifically assigned by the professor, but usually, you have some flexibility in the selection of the subject matter of your paper. Hopefully, there will be enough material on an assigned topic for you to complete a successful paper. If you are selecting your own topic, this may not necessarily be the case. If you are able to choose your own topic, be certain that there is enough material before you commit yourself. It is possible to write a paper that is just one long string of comments and opinions. It won't be a very good paper, however. It will just be a long clothesline of facts and/or opinions strung out for the reader to see. Incidently, you should be very clear in distinguishing between fact and opinion. It is not difficult to recognize facts as facts. A name, a date, or a documented, observed incident is a fact. Many things that are considered to be facts are really opinions. Referring to something that has been written by a prominent person does not make it a fact. It is still just an opinion. There is no problem with including your own opinion or the opinion of others in your writing as long as you indicate it clearly with a footnote. Your paper, however, cannot be a string of quotations.

One area which causes great difficulty to students is the fact that you must give a proper reference to the source of the opinion as well as for any facts which you may include. You must understand what it means to copyright material. A writer who has produced a work has created something of value and that right to that material must be protected. The government provides this protection through the Copyright Office, but you do not have to send your material to Washington to obtain a copyright. The law states that your copyright is created when you first put the material into human readable form. You do not have to file it with the Copyright Office unless you are planning to defend your copyright in a court of law. The cost of obtaining a copyright is very small and the forms are simple to fill out so it is recommended that the writer obtain the copyright once the product is in final form. Human readable form means that a human can read the material without the assistance of another device. This means that if the product is only ever created on a computer disk, for example, it cannot be copyrighted. If you make a printed version of the product then that can be copyrighted. You often see a circle with the letter "c" inside it and the year such as "2000". This means that the work is copyrighted and this was done in the year 2000. Even if you don't put the symbol on your work, it is still copyrighted.

231

The question of fair use of the material is too extensive to discuss here. There are laws concerning the use of material belonging to others and you will often see signs in stores that do copying restricting the material that can be copied.

If you use the words of someone else, you have to give a citation to that work, that is who wrote it, when it was written, the name of the article and the magazine or in the case of a book, the title, the publisher, the place it was published and the year. There are specific forms for this information which must be used and which will not be discussed here. Remember that you cannot just string quotations together and call that a paper. Remember that citing an article or book once in a paper is not enough. You must give the citation every time you quote something from the article.

It is important for your paper to have structure. It may seem obvious, but your paper must have a beginning, a middle and an end. Each of these parts doesn't just happen. Your paper must have more than a topic. It must have a pivotal point or central point which is the focus of the whole paper. The selection of this pivotal point and its substantiation is the key to a successful paper.

The beginning of the paper must have an opening sentence, which sets the tone for the remainder of the paper and states the main point. It should be well written and perhaps revised a number of times.

The middle part of the paper is just that. This is the section in which you put the facts, opinions, etc. you are using to substantiate your premise or main point.

The end is not just the last part of the paper. It is not just where you stop because you ran out of time. It is the summing up, it is the conclusion. It is, in one sense, a rewording of the first part.   Papers have been summarized as having the following steps: you say what you are going to say in the first part, you say it in the middle, and then you say what you said in the conclusion. Too many papers just reach an end. They don't have a proper summary. If you look at a paper that wasn't successful, you will find it probably didn't have a good structure. You may find it didn't have a single key point. While it is possible to support a major point and some minor points in the same paper, you cannot support several major points successfully. You also cannot have a successful paper without a main point.

Simple, clear writing is always the most effective. Writing teachers will tell you that over and over, but somehow it doesn't always seem to "take". If you are asked to do a creative writing assignment, you are often told to write about something you know. Be certain to follow the rules of grammar, spelling and punctuation. I used to keep a little pocket book of 20,000 words next to my typewriter so that I could check the spelling of a word without having to get out my big dictionary. This investment of $1.45 saved me much effort and the embarrassment of having misspelled words in my writing. Now I have a word processing program that has a spell checker which contains most words. In my previous book, I would run each section of the book through the spell checker as I finished it. Now my word processing program underlines in red any word it does not have in its dictionary as I type. It may make suggestions as to the proper spelling. I can choose one of the computer suggestions or I can enter my own change or I can have it skip the word because it is correct but not in the dictionary. It may, for example, be a proper name. The word processing program however, will not spot incorrect uses of a word, such as to, too, and two. You must be very careful that the word you choose from those offered to you by the spell checker is the correct one. Sometimes it gives you a choice which is correctly spelled but not the word you want to use. Also it will not catch mis-spellings which are also a word, for example, "from" and "form" are both words and if you type the wrong one, the spell checker will not catch that error. Spell checkers are not perfect, but they are very helpful.

Be very clear about the rules of grammar and punctuation. Are you writing incomplete sentences? That is a very common error. Are you comfortable with the rules of grammar and the parts of speech? There are many excellent self-instructional books on the rules of grammar, which will help you review or learn these all-important rules for the first time. You don't need to know all of the names for the parts of speech but you need to know the structure of grammar so that you can use the correct form of the word.

233

There are very formal rules for footnotes and bibliographical entries. Manuals have been written which have slightly different forms. Most colleges have adopted one of these manuals as their official style manual. Some departments use different forms, which are related to the forms used by the professional journals for that discipline. Be certain you know the correct form before you type your paper. Be certain you have enough information to complete your citation. A citation is the reference to the source of the information.

Whatever you do, type your paper. This chapter is entitled communication, and the manner in which you present your work is part of this communication. If it is handwritten, dirty etc. you are displaying lack of interest and respect for the course. Some professors will not take a paper unless it is typed. Remember this when you read the chapter on using computers.

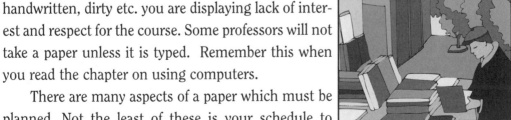

There are many aspects of a paper which must be planned. Not the least of these is your schedule to write the paper. When you are given the assignment date, pretend it is a week earlier and have your paper finished early. You may not be able to get books from the library or find other resource material if you wait until the last minute. It really won't take you any more time to finish it early.

This is by no means a complete description of how to write a paper. It also does not tell you everything you need to know about the art of writing. These are each topics for entire books and even a series of books. This section is intended to point out to you some of the basic points which you must recognize and to direct you to further sources.

Speech and Other Forms of Communication

You communicate with your speech, by the tone of your voice and by body language. Your grammar, the pitch of your voice, and the way you sit are all parts of communication. Listen to yourself on tape. Are you pleasant to listen to? Everyone thinks that the tape distorts their voices but the distortion is far less than we imagine. "That doesn't sound like me," is the instant reaction of everyone when they hear themselves on tape for the first time. It probably is a lot closer to what you sound like than you imagine.

234

What do you sound like? What kind of an impression do you make on others? Poor grammar is translated by the listener into "this person is not very smart." Be smart, be "grammar perfect."

Think of the other qualities you project with your body language. Are you secure, insecure, aggressive, proud, beautiful, etc? Many of your characteristics are projected not by what you say, but by how you say it and your attitude or body language as you say it.

To others, you are what you communicate. Part of the change you must make is to improve your ability to communicate with others.

How to Include Computers in Your Life

Just as computers are a part of many jobs today, so are they an important part of returning to school. Yes, you can still write out answers to questions on tests in long hand, although some schools do make provision for allowing you to type your exams. Exams, however, are the only instance in which many schools accept hand written materials. You may know how to type and plan to use the old typewriter from the attic to get your papers produced. 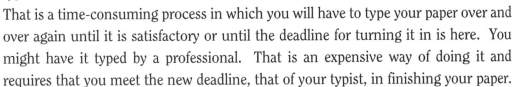 That is a time-consuming process in which you will have to type your paper over and over again until it is satisfactory or until the deadline for turning it in is here. You might have it typed by a professional. That is an expensive way of doing it and requires that you meet the new deadline, that of your typist, in finishing your paper.

The answer is that you learn to use a computer yourself with a sophisticated word processing program such as Word Perfect, Word, or any of the other up to date word-processors. While these programs are somewhat complex, you don't have to learn to use all of their functions from the very beginning. You start with entering and saving the text and then move on from there. You may have to learn to use computers in the new career you are choosing. Start early. Take a course from a computer store or in adult education, or in the school you will be attending. You may be able to use computers provided at the school you will be attending or in your public library until you can afford to buy your own. Remember, though, if you use the school's computer you will be competing with others so don't wait until the last minute to use it. Printers are often not provided for every computer and you will have to queue up for the printer. You may want to buy your own computer, but talk to some computer users if you are not knowledgeable yourself. Don't rush into that expensive purchase without some help and advice. You want to buy the right one for the best price.

Enhance your communication skills for success not only in academic programs but in obtaining a job in your new career.

235

Chapter 20
Studying the Company

O ne evening when I was giving a talk at a local bookstore, a man raised his hand to ask a question. He explained that he was very discouraged. In spite of excellent academic credentials, he was unable to find a job to replace the one he had just left. It was not clear whether there had been down-sizing in his company or whether he had simply been fired. The problem was he couldn't get another job. "I've sent out at least one hundred copies of my resume," he exclaimed "And not a single nibble."

"There were one hundred jobs that were the so much the same that you could use the same resume?" I asked. "I didn't send in for any particular job. I just sent the same resume to one hundred companies and didn't get an answer." was his response.

I am certain you can guess what I told him was the source of his problem. He needed to study the company to which he was applying and the available jobs there that he was able to perform and shape his resume for each job application. He was shocked when I told him this. "You mean that I have to prepare 100 different resumes?" he asked, shocked at the prospect.

"I hope not," I answered, "but you must prepare the resume directed towards the job you are seeking. Even a good resume will do you little good if it is not specific." I didn't say this to him but a resume is like a love letter. You are hoping that the company will fall in love with you sufficiently from your letter that they will at least invite you in for an interview. Would you have a blanket love letter that you would use with every girl you meet? Or even only with those you are serious about. Wouldn't you try to learn everything about the girl before you sent her a love letter? Wouldn't you shape the letter to what you found out about her? Personnel directors often receive hundreds of letters for each advertisement they run. They certainly don't have time to read resumes that are not directed toward a specific job opening. They are not going to put them in any file but the circular one unless you have extraordinary credentials.

How do you determine the company's needs? Look in the newspaper and see what jobs they are advertising. Visit the personnel office of the company and look at the jobs that are posted there. Look in Dun and Bradstreet and other books that do research on the larger companies and rate them. These company biographies often give information about the company activities. From this, you can project the kinds of jobs they might have. You might get the same information from a stock prospectus. What does the company do? How many employees are employed at the location in which you are interested?

238

The more you can find out about the company, the more you can shape your resume to meet its needs.

While this comparison with a love letter is a little extreme, there is a good foundation of truth in it. You can't make a company fall in love with you with a resume that doesn't direct itself to the specific company needs.

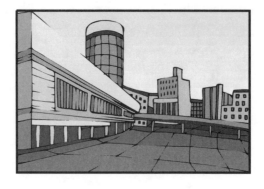

Chapter 21
Summing Up
Yourself
The Resume

*I*n order to resume you must have a resume. That seems like a sentence that one might have thought up for a game of charades or some kind of question in a New York Times crossword puzzle. There really is quite a bit more to the relationship between the two words than an accident or incident, if you will, of spelling.

I must admit that I never thought of the link between the two words, resume used as a noun with the accent omitted in most usages of it and resume, used as a verb. The use of the French word seems so elegant, so polished, so cosmopolitan. It adds a certain element of class to that piece of paper that reduces your life, your successes, your failures and your dreams to a few lines to be interpreted by the reader.

Putting Your Resume Together

A resume is directly related to the importance of the position you are seeking. It is an outline of your experiences, your objectives, your education and your aptitudes. A person applying just for a job does not generally have a resume. He or she fills out an application, of course, but "just a job" does not generally require a resume. A career does require this, whether you are beginning a career, changing careers or continuing your present one. The product you submit as your resume reflects not only your training, your ability and your experiences, but also your attitude toward these things. It is the vehicle by which you sell yourself. To resume is to begin again. It implies that one has started before, made some gains, shown some progress, has taken a respite for whatever reason, and is now ready to continue. This element of continuity is difficult for the person who is seeking their first position but it is still possible.

"How can you get a job if you haven't had a job?" This question is often heard among young people. The problem is equally true for older people who are seeking to change or begin careers later in life. How can you begin a career when you haven't had experience in the area of the new career?"

At no time does a lack of relevant experience seem more like a stone wall than when you are trying to put together your resume. "How can your write a resume when you haven't had any experiences?" The resume creates an impression of you that may determine not only whether or not you get the position you seek, but whether you even get an interview for that position. You must decide what you want to project through this resume. Among a great number of other things you certainly want to project are the old-time virtues of cleanliness and tidiness both of thought and presentation. You may think that you are entering a technical area and such things will not be important but that is not true. The person who selects your resume from a large pile of submissions (or e-mail pile) will certainly be subconsciously influenced by the style of your presentation if not consciously. You want to ensure that your resume is read.

There are certain criteria regarding the appearance of a resume. Some general rules have developed over the years, and whether or not you agree with them, you should follow them. You may have very specific ideas about the appearance of your resume and you may be right, for your particular case. But in almost every instance, the following relationships hold up.

1. A resume should be printed or typed on paper that measures 8 1/2 x 11 inches. Both larger and smaller sheets of paper are just not acceptable.

2. A resume should be perfectly typed with no (absolutely no!) spelling errors or typographical errors. This rule applies even if the position does not include a typing requirement.

3. A resume should be reproduced on a laser printer or on a very high quality copier on good bond paper so that it is almost indistinguishable from the original. You can have your resume printed or bond paper can be used in high quality reproduction equipment. A word processing program and a laser printer can produce a beautiful looking resume. If you do not have this system available for your use, you may find an office supply store or photocopy center that will produce your resume on a computer disk and will make the copies you need for a reasonable price. They will produce additional copies when you need them or make changes for you. You will need originals or very high quality copies. If you submit an original of your resume, don't think it will be returned in a good condition so that it can be used again. It never is. You wouldn't want it to be since that would mean that no one ever looked at it. The most likely is that it won't be returned at all.

4. A resume should be printed on white paper or on a very soft cream color (off-white or ivory) paper. There are many people who will tell you to print your resume on colored paper in order to make it stand out among a pile of other resumes. Although it is important to "stand out," it is more important that you stand out for the right reason. You should stand out because of a certain element of professionalism, because of the classiness of the presentation, rather than for gaudiness unless this somehow fits with the career you have chosen.

241

The resume is often the first and sometimes the only way you are represented to a prospective employer. Be certain that it represents you correctly. If you are moving into a completely new career area, add to your past work experience some examples of things you have done that will support the new career area. Draw on your educational back-ground to reinforce this as well.

Should You Send a Letter?

The answer to the question "Should you send a letter?" is almost always yes. The letter, however, changes with the circumstances.

If you are sending a letter with the resume, it should also be expertly typed on white or off-white 8 1/2 x 11 inch stationery. Mass-produced resumes are marginally acceptable if copied on a good machine, but letters should always be originals. Each company with which you communicate should feel it is the "only one." A multicopied letter is never regarded in the same manner as an original. Would you send a photocopy of a love letter? Again, a computer and high quality printer is a marvelous solution to the multiple letter problem. Each copy is an original. You must determine the name of the contact person at the company, correctly spelled, and with their title. This often can be identified by calling the company. You don't have to go to the department to obtain this information. Often the telephone operator or receptionist can provide it.

There are a number of different types of letters you may write.
- Blind inquiry letter
- Letter in response to position announcement
- Resume letter
- Thank-you letter
- Letter in response to offer
- Resignation letter

The Blind Inquiry Letter

The blind inquiry letter is perhaps the most difficult to write. This letter introduces you to a company and allows you to inquire about open positions that may fit with the talents you describe in the resume portion of the letter. In order to properly write this letter you must know quite a bit about the company and the positions which it may have open now or at a future date. Some positions are never advertised. Positions may be created to make use of available talent. You do not want to eliminate yourself from a possible position with either a totally ambiguous letter from which they could not identify a position for you or an overly specific letter which would limit the positions available to you. The letter should be brief and should state your employment goals, your educational achievements, and a summary of your experience. You don't need to list dates but you should state specifically what you did for previous employers. This letter is usually a one page document.

You can discover a great deal about a company from the reference section of your public library. You may also be able to look back through the want ads of your local paper and review the positions they have had open in the past year. While the same position may not be currently available, such review will establish the type of positions that the company has and possibly a salary level. Never include a salary request in a blind inquiry letter or in a response letter.

Many technologically oriented companies are accepting e-mail inquiries and applications. While this eliminates the question of what paper to use, it does not change the need for you to meet the other specific standards which are discussed in this paper.

Before computers and excellent printers were available to individuals, it was necessary to make a large investment in paper and envelopes to have your letterhead printed. Most businesses made this investment but most individuals decided this was an unnecessary expense. With the advent of superior printer power, letterheads are often printed by the computer as part of the letter that is being produced. It is even 243 possible to add a graphic design to the letterhead.

The format for the letterhead would be:

FIRST NAME MIDDLE INITIAL LAST NAME
Street Address
City, State, Zip Code
Telephone Number
Fax Number
E-mail address

You can experiment with different type fonts and sizes of type until you are satisfied by the look on the page. If you have a logo for your business, you might consider turning that into a graphic but don't get too elaborate unless it suits your business. Remember you are seeking a job with another company. If you are looking for a consulting position, a logo on your letterhead might be very appropriate.

Inquiry Letter

LETTERHEAD

April 6, 2001

Ms. Alice Henderson, Director of Personnel
Atlas Manufacturing, Inc.
555 Main St.
East Lynn, MA 02178

Dear Ms. Henderson

   After working as a teacher for a number of years, I have recently directed my interests toward the training of adults. Currently I am a candidate for the Masters in Human Resource Management degree at the University of Massachusetts, Boston campus.
   Your recent expansion of personnel indicates to me that you will need to expand your training staff. I believe I am the right person to fill your training needs. I have included a resume and will call in a week for an appointment for an interview.

Yours truly,

Harold Edgerton, Jr.

The Response to a Position Announcement Letter

The letter in response to a position announcement, whether it be one you obtain from a placement office or from a newspaper or professional journal, should also be brief, and must either be accompanied by a resume or include the terms of a resume. You have two alternatives here. If the position announcement outlines certain qualifications for the position, you may summarize in your letter those points in your resume which meet these specifications. You may discuss briefly (emphasis on briefly) those aspects of your resume you believe will convince the recipient that he or she should interview you for the position. Alternately, you can write a simpler letter expressing your interest and availability for an interview but this is not as satisfactory. You want to grab the person reading your letter from the beginning and forcing them to pick out the specific matches in your resume with their job announcement does not do that. In either case, you must attach the resume. Your statements should be brief and to the point. Obviously, the grammar should be flawless and the typing should be perfect, even if it is an e-mail.

245

You may state some reasons you are interested in the position or why you feel your background is appropriate. If your resume basically consists of background in non-related fields, you might want to state your reasons for believing that you can fill the position in spite of this limitation. You would not want the reviewer to think that you didn't understand the requirements for the position. In this case, it will be better to write a strong inquiry letter containing some resume elements and basically directed toward the reasons the position interests you and the strengths you will bring to the job.

Letter in Response to Position Announcement

LETTERHEAD

March 4, 2001

Mr. Charles Jordan, Managing Editor
Raspy Dale Free Press
31 Main St.
Happy Dale, PA 44445

Dear Mr. Jordan

I am writing in response to your advertisement for a writer to assume responsibility for the "Happy Doings" column in your weekly paper and to do additional feature writing.

As a freelance writer for the past five years, I have had a number of articles published, many of which can be categorized as human interest. I have a Bachelors degree from Penn State with a major in English, and my studies included a number of courses in journalism. I was editor of the "Campus Capers" column in the Penn State daily paper during my senior year. I have a strong interest in people which led me to many of the subjects who have appeared in my columns.

I am enclosing a resume and copies of three of my most recently published articles. I will provide you with additional samples of my work upon your request.

Yours truly,

Sheri Carpenter

The Resume Letter

The resume letter is one that presents your resume in a directed manner. Key headings from your resume, such as education, experience and goals, are addressed in a less formal manner than in your resume. Neither your complete educational background or work background need be included here. Gaps will not be as noticeable as they may be in a formal resume. Be certain you have not written the resume letter, however, so that it appears there is only one position for which you may be qualified. You may be unknowingly eliminating yourself from another and possibly better position of which you are not aware.

The Thank You Letter

The thank-you letter is more than just something you send to Aunt Tillie to thank her for the birthday present she sent you. It is sent a day or two after an interview. It can be very effective and may cause an interviewer to remember you. It might be the very thing that causes your resume to be pulled out from a pile of resumes after an interview. **247**

Thank You Letter (reduced from actual 8½X11 letter size paper)

LETTERHEAD

April 17, 2001

Mr. Charles Harrison, Manager
Systems Operations Division
IBH Corp,
Peekskill, NY 33333

Dear Mr. Harrison

Thank you for the opportunity to interview for the position of system analyst and for the tour of the IBH operation. Through our discussion, I understand the positive balance that is achieved by the small research department within a large corporation. After reviewing the information packet you gave me, I am quite interested in becoming a part of your project.

Yours truly,
Sid Byte

What If They Make an Offer?

Persistence, something short of "nagging," is vital to obtaining a new position. A very simple letter expressing your appreciation for the interview and continued interest in the position will once more bring your name to the attention of the interviewer.

If you receive an offer from the company, you may have to respond in writing. If you accept the position, you may have certain conditions for that acceptance and they should be listed clearly in the letter. If you decide to reject the position, do it with the idea that you may want a position with that company at a later date. Your letter should be discrete about the reason for your rejection. You should respond to every communication you get from a company except for letters that say no position is open for someone with your qualifications at this time. These are basically form letters and do not require a response. Some sample letters follow.

Acceptance of Offer Letter (reduced from actual 8½X11 letter size paper)

248

LETTERHEAD

January 23, 2001

M_. Patricia McCoy
Super Deluxe Tool Co.
444 Middle St.
Lake Forest, TN 43258

Dear Mr. McCoy

I am pleased to accept your offer of employment as a Supervisor of the Data Entry Department at a salary of $38,500.00

I will give notice to my employer today and report for work on February 20.

I am looking forward to joining Super Deluxe.

Yours truly,
Sandra Downs

Rejection of Offer Letter (reduced from actual 8½X11 letter size paper)

LETTERHEAD

Jan 23, 2001

Mr. Hirum Walker
Ace Tool Co.
1456 Main St.
Lake Forest, IL 43256

Dear Mr. Walker

I have given consideration to your offer of a position in the data processing department. I have received a number of other offers and have decided to accept one which provides me with a more responsible position than you offered.

Thank you for the opportunity to learn about your firm.

Yours truly,

249

How Long is a Resume?

The length of the resume is dictated by its purpose and the amount of information you have to present. Although there is no single resume format, specific areas should be covered. These include biographical information, education, professional goals, experience, military service, public offices held, publications, awards, etc. The arrangement of this information on the page or pages should be clear and easily referenced. There is no absolute format for this, but some suggested forms of resumes are presented in this chapter. Others are to be found in the examples that many on-line employment companies provide.

You may, in fact, need more than one form for your resume. A brief resume is useful as an introduction or as an attachment to a presentation piece or portfolio.'

There are some people who say that no matter what you have done in your life, you should not present a resume that is more than one page long. It is recognized today that this is a ridiculous statement. It may be satisfactory for students who are just graduating from college and have little if any experience but for a professional person it doesn't work at all. There must be a balance between the length of the resume and the information it is presenting. Make it as lean as possible but get the information into the document. There are different length resumes for different purposes.

Brief Resume

Biographical Information

Include name, address, home telephone number, and business telephone number if you will be able to receive a call at this business number.

By law you do not have to include your age or any information which may reveal your age such as dates of graduation.

250

Education

List colleges attended, year graduated (if age is not a problem), and degree(s) received. List advanced study, even if it did not lead to a degree, if it is relevant to the purpose of the resume. Indicate school, year attended (if age is not a problem) and the area studied. You may, for example, call it, "Additional course work in the field of...." List work done to obtain licenses or other credentials.

Goals

Goals (objectives) should be listed on this resume. Short term goals and long term objectives should be included here. Be careful not to cause the person who is reviewing your resume to believe that you will only stay with them only a short time until a more advanced position opens up somewhere else. If there is a clear connection between your present job, your past jobs and the position you seek it may be useful.

Experience

List your current position first. If it is a fairly good one, put in details about what you actually do and your accomplishments in this job. Then pull out your major accomplishment at previous positions. You should give the name of the company and the years for which you worked for them again putting the years in only if age is not a problem. It is sometimes difficult to leave out the dates of employment Include duties in these positions. If you do not have an extensive work background or if it is not relevant to the position you are seeking, you may need to add some "unpaid" work which may be relevant. If you have an extensive work history, present only the last ten years or four positions on this short resume. Indicate other experiences in block form, e.g. 1985-1995 various positions in the retail industry. You will have to include volunteer or unpaid positions to expand this section in the direction of your reputation. You may have to focus on certain aspects of jobs you have held to give evidence of work in the new field. Do whatever you can to add relevant experience in this area.

251

Military Service

Include description of military service.

Publications/ Presentations

Expand your list to include more than just your last two year's work. Do not hesitate to include reports which were circulated inside your company if you can prove that you did the work.

Awards

This may be included only if the awards are significant.

Public Office

Include if it is a responsible position.

CHARLES HARRIS
543 Maple Street
Miami, Florida 33290
Home Telephone   (305) 987_6543
e-mail charlieH@AOL.com <mailto:charlieH@AOL.com>

POSITION DESIRED
A position of responsibility in a corporate training department that will allow me to train adults using techniques I have learned both through formal training in education and through experience in teaching.

EDUCATION

1995- 1987	Nova University, Fort Lauderdale, Fl. M.S. Degree Major: Human Resource Management
1980-1984 Education	Florida Atlantic University, Boca Raton, Fl. B.S. Degree Major: Science

EXPERIENCE

1989-present	Dade County School System, Miami, Florida Middle School science teacher in three Dade County Middle Schools. Developed instructional material in science for seventh grade students, a remedial mathematics program for eighth grade students, and started a science club program in two schools.
1984-1988	United States Infantry Officer Tactical Training Officer, Port Belvoir, Virginia highest rank held was Captain

Expanded Resume

The expanded resume will include everything in the Short Resume and more. This was a more significant category when the style was to have only a single page for most resumes.

Biographical Data

You may add information about hobbies, interests, travel, languages spoken, etc. This will give the reviewer a more complete picture of you.

Goals

A more complete discussion of objectives may be included on this resume.

Experience

You may include all the positions you have held and the accomplishments and responsibilities with regard to these positions. You may expand the listing of volunteer positions, especially if they are related t0 your new career goals. But don't just pad things.

A few additional comments for all types of resumes are:

1. If you don't want your current employer to know you are seeking a new position, you should indicate this on your resume or in the accompanying letter and be discrete about receiving calls at your office. You certainly would not type your letter on your company letterhead.

2. Don't use company time to prepare your letters and resumes. If you have no other access to a computer and your boss has indicated that you may use your office computer on your off hours such as lunchtime don't leave a copy of this work on your hard-drive. Invest in a disc and take your material home. Your boss has the right to see everything on your computer.

3. Don't include the names of references on your resume. You may indicate that references are available upon request. Do get permission from the individuals before you use their names, make certain they really know you and understand the type of position you are seeking, Find out what they are going to say before you have them submit a reference for you, and be certain they will tell you what they will say. I have checked on people's references at times and discovered that the person can give only a bad reference or doesn't even remember the applicant. Most companies have a policy that will allow the personnel department to only confirm that a person worked there during a specific period of time.

Don't short-change your self in preparing your resume. Read it over to determine if you are clear and competent. Would you hire yourself if you were the personnel manager? If you would not, you need to revise that resume..

Chapter 22
Selling Yourself: The Interview

How to Prepare for the Interview

For some reason, I still remember the way I dressed for my first job interview (which, I might add, did lead to my first job). I wore a navy blue shirtwaist dress with a white collar, medium heels, nylon stockings, and carried white gloves. I had all the confidence which my seventeen years, and the fact that I was going to college in the fall, could give me. No matter how good or bad the job, it was only temporary. I filled out an application, talked first to someone in the personnel department and then to the woman for whom I would work, and was hired.

The white gloves will give you a clue as to how long ago that job interview took place. The simplicity of the process I went through is almost as out of fashion as the white gloves. Of course, I was applying for only a low-paying job, probably at the minimum wage which was $1.00 per hour at the time. I told you it was a long time ago. Obtaining a position at the professional level today often has all the simplicity of a NASA space launch compared to the process I went through on my first adventure in the world of work. Because obtaining a new position may involve several creative aspects, you may be more successful if you can get yourself "involved" rather than sitting back as if you consider yourself to be on trial. I realize this is much easier to write about than it is to do.

Although interviewing can bring terror to the hearts of otherwise cool individuals, it is an important part of a career change. The fact that you have made it to the interview means that your resume has survived some level of inspection. Now you will have to sell yourself to the interviewer. Interviewers understand your nervousness. They had to interview for their jobs also. It is important that you minimize your nervousness. This is especially true if the position you are seeking will be somewhat stressful. In order to be successful at presenting yourself in a job-seeking session you have to realize the complexities of placement today for many professional-level positions.

Hiring has become an extraordinarily complicated business phenomenon closely related to firing. Not only are there agencies specializing in placement, but some specialize in "outplacement" by helping individuals, who have been terminated, to face the future. I have done a great deal of hiring over the years and find that I am conscious more and more of the prospect of terminating someone, even during the initial interview. I find myself thinking what it would be like to fire that person. It is almost like writing the divorce settlement as part of the marriage proposal process, but apparently that also is being done today. There are so many federal regulations and lawsuits for one reason or another, that the person doing the hiring has to take extraordinary measures to protect himself or herself in the hiring and firing processes. In most cases the interviewer, unless this is his or her profession, is not comfortable with the process of interviewing. He or she is concerned that something will not be revealed in the interview that will ultimately result in a serious problem if the person is hired. The interview process, then, must produce a great deal more information than you might anticipate in order to ensure that sufficient data is available for the decision-making process. This leads to some very complex interview techniques, of which you must be aware if you are going to successfully compete in the career market. In some cases, the hiring process has become extremely creative, as well as lengthy. One of my many hats is that of president of a corporation that, among other things, develops and conducts assessment centers.

256

The Assessment Center

An assessment center is not a place, but a happening. It can involve the assessment of several hundred people at one time or a small number of interviewees for similar positions. It can happen in a few hours, it may take two or more consecutive days to be completed, or the sessions may be separated by various time periods.

The assessment center may include some kind of written testing on the part of the interviewee. If you go through one which has been developed by "The A. & R. Burke Corporation" it will contain several sessions in which you must perform some kind of job simulation activity and several group interaction activities. Many assessment centers contain some psychological testing and some intelligence testing. Others stress role playing. The real key to success in an assessment center is "letting yourself go," participating fully in the exercises. Show that you are outgoing —a true leader —but don't be obnoxious. Be a team leader and a team player at the same time.

If we review for a moment the process of developing a set of assessment center 257 activities for a particular professional position, you may better understand the rationale behind the hiring process for that position.

First of all, the person or team who is doing the hiring generally is not certain of what they are doing. Certain questions are always present for them. "Am I selecting the right person?" "Does this person have some flaw I have overlooked?" "Is there some characteristic central to the position that I have overlooked?" If you understand where the interviewer is coming from, you will have a more successful interview.

When we are developing a custom-tailored assessment center, certain parameters must be established at the beginning, and this process often reveals some hidden agendas on the part of the individual(s) who will select the successful candidate. The characteristics required for the position must be determined by the group which is doing the hiring and these characteristics will often have little to do with the advertised requirements for the position. There will be certain minimum requirements for education and experience which will be advertised or posted in a job bulletin. Those who are selecting the individual are interested in that person's ability to perform on the job, to be simultaneously a leader of others and a follower for them, if they are to be the supervisor. There will be individuals in the department with whom this person will have to interact and these will have "known" characteristics with which the person must interface. The person doing the hiring is interested in knowing the work habits of the interviewees. Are they able to learn new tasks quickly? Are they dependable? Are they imaginative? Different characteristics are important in different positions. Although many make this mistake, executives should not surround themselves with individuals who all have the same characteristics. Every company needs a successful mix of professionals. These characteristics are what must be revealed during the interview, or more rigorous assessment center, as well as the basic job knowledge.

Although you may think you are being hired for your individual prior achievements, one of the factors that your prospective employer may be looking as is your ability to be a team player.

Basic Elements of an Interview

258

Let us think your way through some basic elements of an interview. Although I did write that you should not act as though you think you are on trial, you are indeed being judged on the basis of the interview. You are being judged on the basis of your appearance and your behavior, on the basis of what you say and do, on your attitudes and expressions and on the basis of what you don't say or don't do. There is no right or wrong answer for which you can prepare before the interview. The person who hires you is the one who determines which answers are right or wrong with regard to a question. Think about it for a moment. Suppose you are able to fool the interviewer and tell him what you think he or she wants to hear. Suppose you present a self that is very different from what you are really like. Suppose you conceal a very different personality from the person who is hiring you. Are you going to want to perform in the new position in the resulting false manner that your superior is going to expect of you? Be careful not to fool yourself in this process. There are times, however, when you will find it necessary to present something in a manner that compensates for some unreasonable or prejudicial position on the part of the person conducting the interview.

Although there are no "right answers" you can learn ahead of time there are certain guidelines we can develop together that will be useful when preparing for an interview.

It may seem to you that you are most successful in obtaining a job when you don't really need it. You may think that this is just luck, when in fact it happens because you are more relaxed and have more confidence in yourself.

Knowledge of a Company

One very important aspect of the interview is knowledge of the company. You may not be able to find out a great deal about the position which is open, but you will certainly be able to get information from books in the reference section of your library or from the personnel office of the company. Is it a large company? Is it self-owned or part of a conglomerate? Does it have offices in other parts of the country? Is it related to other companies? How many employees does it have? How many years has the company been in business? What is the financial status of the company? Has it just had a reorganization or a merger? You can't really ask if the company is solvent, but if there has been some statements about finances in the newspaper, for example, you might want to ask about them. When the interviewer asks if you have any questions about the company, don't be shy. Ask whatever you want to know, exercising a reasonable amount of prudence.

These elements may be important in your final decision as to whether or not you will take the job, and they will also give you a knowledge base from which to work in your interview. Learn these things before you even apply to the company.

Suppose you are called for an interview. Your education and experience have probably already been identified in the resume. If you are seeking a career position, these characteristics will already have been reviewed in a screening process. This process may have been separated from the interview by only a short period of time or by several weeks, but this differentiation in time will generally exist.

Let us assume there will be one or more interviews which you will have to suc-

259

cessfully complete for a certain position, but that there is not a formal assessment center. There are many components for which you will have to be prepared.

Showing the Right Attitude

You must agree with yourself. You are trying to get a position, not make a social statement. This may seem to be a ridiculous statement, but many people lose touch with their purpose in the process of establishing something else, such as an excuse for not getting the position, or to satisfy an unconscious fear that they will get the job but not be able to perform. A man who will not get a haircut or wear a tie, or a woman who wears tight pants or a plunging neckline to an interview for a business position is not thinking about winning that position. They are trying to make a social statement, and perhaps are subconsciously setting up a defense for rejection by not playing by the rules.

Your appearance is very important and must be correlated to the position you are seeking. Review again the previous chapter which addresses this issue. This may or may not change according to the area of the country in which the position is located. People from outside of the state are often not aware of the fact that most professional people in Florida dress in the same manner as people in New York including wearing wool in the winter. They seem to believe that cruise wear is the order of the day in Florida business offices, but this is not true. Study not only what is being worn in the general industry to which you are applying for a position, but in that particular company, and in that particular job.

Some colleges and companies are very "tweedy," while others are characterized by business suits. I do not use the term "suit" only with respect to men. The acceptance of the skirted suit, the ensemble or the jacketed dress as a uniform for the professional woman, has been very rapid. A tailored dress may also be worn, especially in warmer weather, but everywhere I go I see suits.

260

Creating the Right First Impression

The first impression you make on the interviewer is with your appearance. Although the specific items of clothing will obviously be different, some of the standards will be the same for both men and women. Unless the position has a special characteristic that must be taken into account such as the lead singer in a rock band, you should dress fairly conservatively in quiet, well-fitting clothing. A suit, skirted for women, is always a good choice. If the weather is warm, women may wear tailored dresses, but men should still wear suits. I do realize that there is a movement away from the suit as a newly-found uniform for women, but it is still a good choice for a job interview. Although a sports jacket might be acceptable in some situations, matching pants and jacket will be generally more effective. Colors should also be conservative unless you have some very good reason for choosing something else. Attractive applicants are selected more often than those who are unattractive.

Please note that I did not say beautiful. Not everyone can be beautiful, and standards for beauty are different. Most people can be attractive, however. Such things as good haircuts and attractive, business-like hairdos, well-fitting, appropriate, and well-coordinated clothing in fairly neutral colors and well-kept shoes add to that attractive image. A woman's make-up will be determined partly by what she generally wears. It should not look as though she were going out for the evening after the interview, but I have never subscribed to the theory that a woman in business should wear no make-up. I have always believed that make-up should be attractive but not obvious. As mentioned in the previous section on appearance, things like dandruff on the shoulder or broken, dirty fingernails loom large in an interview, although, they are totally unimportant in most work situations. You create an image in an interview. Be certain that your appearance adds favorably to that image.

Games Interviewers Play

You may have to interact with one or more interviewers on one or more separate occasions. In the later sessions, the interview may be more complex, but the factors you must remember will be the same. When considering an interview, I cannot help but remember some of the techniques the police are said to use when questioning suspects. The typical TV scene will be a poorly lit room in the station house with a naked bulb hanging from the ceiling. One detective will be nasty, relentlessly questioning the suspect; the other will be the good guy, who will interfere and play the role of friend to the criminal. The criminal responds to the kindness by telling the nice officer where he hid the body or the jewels, etc.

Interviewers don't play quite the same games, but they are dedicated to getting you to reveal things about yourself that you don't want to reveal. You may believe you will not reveal these things, but the skilled interviewers can get you to do it. Remember, you won't give a good interview if you do not interact to some degree. You cannot just answer with a monosyllabic "yes" or "no" or "I don't know." You cannot plead the fifth amendment and still get hired. You should be aware of this if there is a particular skeleton you want to keep in your closet. In a recent assessment cen-

ter we were planning, one of the people from the company told us that he was going to use a psychological evaluation in addition to the material we had developed. This apparently was designed to reveal all sorts of things, such as whether or not the person being considered was an alcoholic. It seemed a little extreme to all of us, but this was what the psychologist had told the company he could obtain through his evaluations. I include this only to give you a sense of the kind of things companies are worried about. Drug testing is required by many companies. If you are not willing, based on general principles you won't get hired.

Many locations can be used for interviewing, depending on the level of the position, but some, if not all, of the interview will be in an office. If the person who is doing the interview does not come out of the office or at least to the door of the office to greet you, take it as a general indicator that the position is not a very high one, regardless of the title. There are three general seating patterns in most offices, and the choice is up to the interviewer. Do not assume a seat until you see where the interviewer will sit. The three patterns are:

1. The interviewer sits at his or her desk. You sit in a chair in front or at the side of

the desk. If the interviewer assumes a seat at the desk and there is no chair near the desk, ask if you can move one to a convenient position. If there is blinding sunlight in your eyes, move your chair slightly. The situation may be staged to see if you have initiative. It is appropriate to have some, but don't have so much that you take the boss's chair.

2. You both sit at a table. This format will be more relaxing than having the interviewer at the desk, because you will be in a peer simulation role here. In the previous example, the desk established the pecking order immediately. You could not doubt for a minute who was "boss," who was in charge. At the position at the table, the seating pattern does not establish who is in charge unless there is a very definite "head of the table" position. Some people have round tables in their offices so that role definition will not be predetermined by the seating. Again, see where the interviewer sits and select a seat from which you can talk clearly without having to sit at an awkward angle to see him or her.

3. The third position is one in which you have comfortable chairs and/or a comfortable sofa. Again your position is dictated by the position which the interviewer takes. If he/she chooses the chair, sit on the end of the sofa which is nearest the chair. If he/she chooses the sofa, don't sit next to him/her. Sit on the other piece of furniture. This arrangement is intended to make you feel very relaxed. If you are a woman wearing an appropriate length skirt, do not allow your skirt to slip up a few inches if you are sitting on the couch. Some pieces of furniture cause that to happen because the seat is too deep. After you have chosen your position, think about the way you are sitting. Body language is extremely important. Your body language may be signalling things you wouldn't dream of saying. What you do with your hands and feet are probably the most important thing. Moving excessively, or tapping your hands or feet may indicate that you are terribly nervous. Never play with your face, your nose, your ears, your hair, etc. Try not to touch them at all. Don't play with jewelry or watches, and for heaven's sake, don't look at your watch. Time should not be important to you in the middle of an interview. You may be signalling the interview is a waste of time for you or you have something better to do, like another interview, and are running late.

Interview Stages

There are generally four stages to an interview. The warm-up time during which you and the interviewer become comfortable with each other is first. Although this is important, don't get so carried away with friendliness that you forget you are there to obtain a position to begin your new career.

During the second stage, you and the interviewer will exchange information. The way you phrase the information you give the interviewer will be part of your selling job. You can reveal some of your knowledge about the company during this process. Choose your words carefully to maximize the things you tell about yourself. Don't talk too much, but don't resort to monosyllables either.

The third stage usually focuses on a specific position or on a general set of positions. Don't hesitate to appear interested if you are. Remaining reserved may give the interviewer the idea that you are not interested in the position. Don't be afraid to inquire about such details as salary range at this point. People sometimes are reluctant to discuss money, but this is an important part of any position. Certain other things should be left until a specific offer is made. You don't need to discuss the retirement package when you are in the middle of a first interview. You should, however, discuss it before you finally take the position, along with the question of raises and promotion policy, medical benefits, educational benefits and other things which will concern you if you take the position. Terminating the interview can be a somewhat difficult process. Try to be confident. Ask any questions which you may still have and watch for the cues that the interviewer considers the interview to be over. You now know more about each other than when you began the interview, and the leave-taking may be friendlier than it was at the beginning. Of course, if the interview didn't go well it may be even more strained. It is sometimes difficult to know if you are the cause of any tenseness on the part of the interviewer. It may be the garlic he had for lunch or the meeting he is on his way to with his boss which causes him to have a sour look. Don't forget to send the thank-you letter.

While the four stages seem simple enough, there are a number of do's and don't's to be remembered.

Do's and Don'ts of Interviewing

Don't get caught up in telling stories or anecdotes. You should talk of course and do more than just give monosyllabic answers to the questions which you are asked, but don't get carried away in little stories. This is especially symptomatic of women returning to work after a long absence. It is perhaps more accepted with men who traditionally tell old war stories. To some degree, you have to follow the lead of the interviewer.

If you have a friend who will role-play with you, use him or her to check you out for your body language and habits. Arrange set-ups for an interview using the three seating patterns described above. Have the person ask you all sorts of questions and note your responses. While your friend may not be able to judge the effectiveness of your responses, he or she will be able to take note of all the things you do that may add or subtract from the interview.

Don't have garlic or onions for lunch. Don't have a beer or a drink, either. Don't wear strong perfume and don't smoke even if the interviewer invites you to. Many offices are non-smoking theses days. If that is a problem for you, check on company policy before the interview.

While I do encourage honesty, there is a limit to what the interviewer is entitled to know. Certain questions may be discriminatory, and a violation of the law. You do not have to answer these types of questions and can say as much in the nicest of terms.

In spite of the illegality of it, some interviewers do not hesitate to ask questions about your age or, in the case of women, if you are expecting a baby. You do not have to answer these questions, but it is not necessarily advisable to bang the interviewer over the head with the illegality of the questions. Discrimination is a reality in spite of the laws. You must fight it, but the interview room is not always the best place. Don't answer a question you don't want to answer, or to which the interviewer is not entitled to the answer. Just don't get around to it.

Because you will be either changing careers or returning to work after a number of years' absence, you will undoubtedly be asked why you are looking for the job for which you are being interviewed. There may be questions about gaps in your employment record or about your selection of the new field. While the interviewer may indeed be looking for answers to which he or she is not legally entitled, the questions are natural. You may never know the real reason for the questions. The questioner may be looking for a new career, himself. Don't be overly sensitive about such questions, and prepare in advance a response that satisfies you both and the interviewer.

Preparing for the Questions

Sometimes the interviewer may ask questions that seem to come out of the *Dictionary of Occupational Titles*, such as, "Are you interested in people, data or things?" "Will you be able to travel?" "Do you like to travel?" or, " What will you do if your children get sick?"

Other questions seem to have been gleaned from a psychological exam. "What kind of a boss do you like to work for?", or alternately, "what style of leadership do you like to assume?" "What are your strengths?", "What are your weaknesses?" "Do you like 'detail' work?" "If you could have any job in the company, what would you choose?" "Why?" "What are your career goals?" "What plans do you have for the next five years?" "Ten years?" "If you could change anything in the company what would it be?"

Sometimes the interviewer will ask you about something on your application which is of interest to him personally. It may be a hobby you have, or a trip you have taken, or the place where you were born or went to school. In South Florida, for example, we always ask people where they are from when we meet them. In New York we generally talk about the transportation we take to work and the hardships we experience (subway breakdowns, LIRR strikes etc.). In Boston, although my contacts may have been too narrow, the conversation seemed to run to skiing, sailing, being stuck on the bridge to Cape Cod and remodeling old houses. I am certain that other regions have their favorite questions. Remember that in the case when the interviewer would be your future boss rather than a professional interviewer, the inter-

266

viewer may also be a little nervous and may be trying to make some small talk to relax both of you.

You have to remember that not all interviewers are nice. The person doing the interview may have many discriminatory attitudes. He or she may want a person who is clearly identified as being the traditional "type" for the position and reject applicants who do not fit a pre-determined idea.

The person who is changing careers, especially at midlife, or is coming back into a profession after a lengthy absence generally does not fit a pre-determined model. Some recent college graduates will find themselves in the same position. There may be many rather pointed questions directed toward him or her. Some of these questions may be very insulting, such as:

- What happened, didn't you do well in your other field?
- Do you think you will be able to get back in the swing after your long vacation? (Raising four children is some vacation.)
- What makes you think you can do this job? (A degree in the field and work experience in other areas.)
- Aren't you a little old to be trying something new?
- This isn't a retirement position, you know.
- I suppose you are going to have to take a lot of time off to take care of your children?
- What do you think about women's lib?
- Did your wife talk you into getting a new job?

267

You may find yourself in the position of having to make a response to questions which are just as improper and just as rudely asked as the previous samples. Although you may be quite angry about the whole situation, you will also have to be ready to respond. One technique is to examine your resume and your life situation (man or woman, in a new career or returning to work, etc.) and make a list of all the nasty questions you anticipate might be asked. Sort these into categories such as age, gaps in your resume, the fact that you are changing careers, your choice of the new career, selection of the particular position, health, family responsibilities, etc. You should prepare general categories of responses to these questions. Refusal to answer, of course, may be one of your choices. Remember, no matter how angry discrimination may make you, you are trying to get a position, not win a battle. You do that after you get the position.

Questions You Should Ask

While the interview is generally considered to be a period in which you respond to questions which are asked of you, you can use it to find out some things about the position for which you are applying. Many interviewers will not necessarily know all the details concerning the health and retirement plans which will apply to you, or the policy on vacations or personal days for people in your category. They may not even know the exact salary scheduled for the position, but it does no harm to ask about the salary range. If the interviewer will

268 be your supervisor, you may ask questions about the work, possibly using the job description as well as questions about the way in which you will function in the office, and about your relationship to the people with whom you will be working. This is information you will need before you can make a decision to accept the position if it is offered. You should not seem overly concerned about a particular aspect of the position that you do not care for, or the interviewer may become negative toward you. Wait until you are offered the position and then negotiate the aspects of the position that displease you. You will be in a better position to do so at that time.

Now I am going to tell you to do the impossible. Relax. Everybody is nervous in an interview to some degree, but the higher the level of the position, the more relaxed and in control you must seem. Although you must be relaxed, you must simultaneously try to be aware of the impact every move you make and every word you say will have on the interviewer. This certainly seems like an impossible undertaking, but it is the task that has been set for you.

It is often said that you get a job offer (and the same goes for a new position) when you are not looking for it and this is frequently true. The point is that you are relaxed when you are not looking for a new position, while this is certainly not the case if you care very much whether you get it. This caring may make you so nervous that you eliminate yourself from the competition.

Stress is a fact of the modern world and the person who is going to survive will have to be able to handle it well. If you cannot function in the interview, the interviewer may well be justified in assuming that you will not be able to survive in the new job. Minimize your stress by mentally acting out many of the steps you will go through ahead of time.

Chapter 23
What If They Make an Offer

*I*ronically, the next to the worst thing to not getting an offer is getting one and having to make a decision whether or not to accept it. Selecting that first position when you are attempting to make a career change is a difficult decision. You have decided to make the change in your life. You have chosen a career and you have gone out and sought a new position. You are probably still asking yourself the question "Am I doing the right thing, have I chosen the right career?" Now you have to ask not only this, but also, "Is this the right job and should I accept it?" If only we were blessed with the ability to see the future once in a while, such questions might be simplified.   Selecting a new job is a little bit like selecting a marriage partner. Is this the right person? If you wait, will a better choice come along? Maybe, maybe not.

Evaluating an Offer

Just as many people are left waiting for the right knight or princess to come riding along, applicants frequently are left waiting for the right position to open up. On the other hand, you might decide too quickly, and take a position just because it was available. I always wonder about a certain position I once accepted when another seemed impossible to get. I had signed a contract for the first position, and the one I preferred was offered to me a few weeks later. I did not want to break a contract, but

I have always wondered what would have happened in my life if I had taken the second position. Perhaps it would have been better, perhaps it would not. I will never know. Life is full of "what ifs." The important thing is to make the best possible decision using all the information at your disposal. Don't let inertia set in. Don't let fear stop you and don't spend your days saying "If only...."

There really is no way to be certain whether you should take a particular position or not. The answer will be different in each person's case. There are, however, a number of questions you can ask yourself. You will have to base your final judgment on the answers to these and other questions which may occur to you. In the end, you will have to make the final decision on the basis of your intuition . . . your feelings. There is an element of luck in every choice and in every decision you make. The key question seems to be concerned not only with the "present" aspects of the job but also with its "future." Travelers Insurance Company used to have an ad describing a gentleman who turned down a position with the newly founded insurance company in 1864. Looking back, the ad claims, the gentleman appears to have been shortsighted. Worried about the economy, he kept his job selling blacksmith supplies. I'm not so certain he was shortsighted. Not everyone is emotionally prepared to take risks. Perhaps selling blacksmith supplies was the best position for him at that time. Selecting the new position can only be made after a great deal of soul searching. Ask yourself some of the following questions:

- Does the position seem to have a future?
- Will it lead me to the next step on my projected career ladder?
- Will the position give me good experience?
- Does the company have a good reputation?
- Does the salary seem fair for the position considering my experience and education?
- Do I like the environment in which I will be working?
- Do I think I can do the work?
- Will you "feel good" about doing the work or having that title or position?
- What is the reaction of my family and friends to the job offer? You don't have to

take their advice, but it is important to involve those who care for you in the decision.

- Will I have to travel, work overtime or unusual hours? How do I feel about that? Am I a night owl or an early riser? Will I be safe coming home at that time?
- Is the position the kind of work I have been seeking?
- Will it give me an opportunity to "get in" to a company which could provide me with the kind of position I really want?
- Will I have to move?
- Will I be able to continue my educational program?
- Do I have any prospects with other companies which might better fit with my goals?
- Have I been out of work and therefore need the job? How long have you been looking?
- Will the specific tasks which I will have to do for the position interest me? Will I be quickly bored?
- How will I get to the new job? Is the commute impossible? Do i have a safe car?
- What will I do if I don't take the position?
- If I turn down this position do I think the company will make me an offer for the job I want at a later date?
- What other job in that company would I prefer?
- What other job in that company am I qualified for?
- Are there any other immediate prospects?
- Will working in this position for a while enable me to get the job I want with another company? Will the experience be valuable?
- have you gotten any other offers? What are the odds you will get other offers?

273

You may want to review some of the problems you have had with jobs in the past. How can you avoid having them repeated in the new position? Are they likely to reappear if you take this position? What do your family and friends think about the offer? Discuss it with those individuals whom you know are not jealous of you or opposed to your change of careers. Do they understand you pretty well? Are they sympathetic to your goals?

Suppose you have had two interviews with companies. Both seem promising. For some reason you would prefer the position at Company A, but the offer comes first from Company B. There is no way that you can put off giving Company B an immediate answer. What do you do, besides chewing your nails, that is?

There are several schools of thought on this question.

1. You can accept the offer from company B. An offer in the hand is worth two in the bush. The second offer may never come.

2. You can turn down the offer from Company B and wait for the offer from Company A. It may not come, but then again, it may come.

3. You can try to get a little time from Company B in order to give them an answer. Remember that they won't like thinking they were your second choice and you may be jeopardizing your future at company B.

4. You can talk to the person from Company A and indicate that you have a viable offer from another company, that you would be interested in considering an offer from them and that you wonder if they are going to make such an offer to you soon. This may blow all of your chances with company A, but if you were going to take company B's offer anyway, that won't matter. It may push Company A into making an offer to you or they may decide they don't want to compete. They may have decided not to make you an offer anyway. This would be suicidal to try if you didn't have a genuine offer of a position from Company B.

Giving Notice to Your Present Employer

After you have made the decision to take the new position you will have to give notice to your current company. Although you may be relieved to be leaving your present position, you cannot make that apparent. Don't tell them what you think of them and the way they have treated you, unless it was great. You will need references from that position for many years. Be sure to leave them with adequate notice and on good terms. Don't tell your boss off, for example, even though you feel he deserves it. Get a letter of recommendation before you leave. It may be useful later.

Mentally prepare yourself for the new position. Have problems arisen in other positions you have held over the years? Have you had

274

problems with co-workers, bosses, punctuality or other things? Think about these things honestly and try to avoid the same problems in your new position. Beginning a new career won't solve your problems if you fall back into patterns that have caused problems for you before. Go back and review the lists you made in chapters two and three.

It will be important for you to fit into the new position while being identified for your abilities. This means fitting in with the people with whom you will be working. It means looking as though you belong in the company. You may need some new items in your wardrobe to look the part you must play in the new position. It means learning your new job quickly and acting with confidence. A willingness to learn is an important asset to bring to your new position.

You should also approach your first position in your new career with a fresh outlook and enthusiasm. Act with the confidence that comes with years of experience, even though it may have been in a different position. You should be excited. It is a fresh future for you and for your family.

Chapter 24
Don't Stop Now

Y ou have taken the first step. You have begun to think about a new career. It is possible for you to have a new career. It is possible for everyone. We only live once and it is important to get some satisfaction from your daily experiences. Your new career may be the heart of your daily experiences. It is important to have pride in yourself and what you do for a living.

You may be looking for a new career because you are just getting out of school. You may not have taken a major in college which was directly connected to the career you desire.

You may be forced to find a new position because your present work area is being phased out by technology. You may have identified a new career area that did not exist in earlier years. You may be thinking about pursuing a dream you have had since childhood. Study the career area carefully. Find a position in that area for which you can prepare yourself. Be realistic about whether or not you will be able to find a position in the new field at a salary you can live on.

You may have identified certain training you will need in order to obtain the position you want within the new career area. You may have to make adjustments in your family life for a period of time. You may have to take a temporary cut in income or you may have to increase your workload. You may have to ask others for help. You may have to borrow money. You may have to go back to school. You may have to do many things that will be hard for you, but the final goal will be worth it.

You took the first step when you picked up this book. Don't stop now. Get busy. Make your lists. Make time available to work on the tasks you have identified. Don't let anyone stop you. Plan it and do it. You are doing it for yourself.

Appendix

Explanation of Data, People, and Things

This section has been taken from the *Dictionary of Occupational Titles*, 4th edition, printed 1977 by the U. S. Department of Labor, Division of Employment and Training.

Much of the information the Dictionary publishes is based on the premise that every job requires a worker to function in some degree to data, people, and things. These relationships are identified and explained below. They appear in the form of three listings arranged in each instance from the relatively simple to the complex in such a manner that each successive relationship includes those that are simpler and excludes the more complex.

The identifications attached to these relationships are referred to as worker functions, and provide standard terminology for use in summarizing exactly what a worker does on the job. As each of the relationships to people represents a wide range of complexity, resulting in considerable overlap among occupations, their arrangement is somewhat arbitrary and can be considered a hierarchy only in the most general sense.

A job's relationship to data, people, and things can be expressed in terms of the lowest numbered function and together indicate the total level of complexity at which the worker performs. The fourth, fifth, and sixth digits of the occupational code numbers reflect relationships to data, people, and things, respectively. Only those relationships which are occupationally significant in terms of the requirements of the job are reflected in the code numbers. The incidental relationships which every worker has to data, people, and things, but which do not seriously affect successful performance of the essential duties of the job, are not reflected.

These digits express a job's relationship to data, people, and things by identifying the highest appropriate function in each listing as reflected by the following table:

DATA 4th digit	PEOPLE 5th digit	THINGS 6th digit
0 Synthesizing	0 Mentoring	0 Setting-Up
1 Coordinating	1 Negotiating	1 Precision Working
2 Analyzing	2 Instructing	2 Operating-Controlling
3 Compiling	3 Supervising	3 Driving-Operating
4 Computing	4 Diverting	4 Manipulating
5 Copying	5 Persuading	5 Tending
6 Comparing	6 Speaking-Signaling	6 Feeding-Offbearing
	7 Serving	7 Handling
	8 Taking Instructions-Helping	

Definitions of Worker Functions

Data: Information, knowledge, and conceptions related to data, people, or things, obtained by observation, investigation, interpretation, visualization, and mental creation. Data are intangible and include numbers, words, symbols, ideas, concepts, and oral verbalization.

0. Synthesizing: Integrating analyses of data to discover facts and/or develop knowledge concepts or interpretations.

1. Coordinating: Determining time, place, and sequence of operations or action to be taken on the basis of analysis of data; executing determination and/or reporting on events.

2. Analyzing: Examining and evaluating data. Presenting alternative actions in relation to the evaluation is frequently involved.

3. Compiling: Gathering, collating, or classifying information about data, people, or things. Reporting and/or carrying out a prescribed action in relation to the information is frequently involved.

4. Computing: Performing arithmetic operations and reporting on and/or carrying out a prescribed action in relation to them. Does not include counting.

5. Copying: Transcribing, entering, or posting data.

6. Comparing: Judging the readily observable functional, structural, or compositional characteristics (whether similar to or divergent from obvious standards) of data, people, or things.

281

People: Human beings, also animals dealt with on an individual basis as if they were human.

0. Mentoring: Dealing with individuals in terms of their total personality in order to advise, counsel, and/or guide them with regard to problems that may be resolved by legal, scientific, clinical, spiritual, and/or other professional principles.

1. Negotiating: Exchanging ideas, information, and opinions with others to formulate policies and programs and/or arrive at decisions, conclusions, or solutions, jointly.

2. Instructing: Teaching subject matter to others, or training others (including animals) through explanation, demonstration, and supervised practice, or making recommendations on the basis of technical disciplines.

3. Supervising: Determining or interpreting work procedures for a group of workers, assigning specific duties to them, maintaining harmonious relations among them, and promoting efficiency. A variety of responsibilities is involved in this function.

4. Diverting: Amusing others. (Usually accomplished through the medium of stage, screen, television, or radio.)

5. Persuading: Influencing others in favor of a product, service, or point of view.

6. Speaking-Signaling: Talking with and/or signaling people to convey or exchange information. Includes giving assignments and/or directions to helpers or assistants.

7. Serving: Attending to the needs of animals or the needs, requests and expressed or implicit wishes of people. Immediate response is involved.

8. Taking Instructions-Helping: Helping applies to "non-learning" helpers. No variety of responsibility is involved in this function.

Things: Inanimate objects as distinguished from human beings, substances or materials; machines, tools, equipment and products. A thing is tangible and has shape, form, and other physical characteristics.

282

0. Setting up: Adjusting machines or equipment by replacing or altering tools, jigs, fixtures, and attachments to prepare them to perform their functions, change their performance, or restore their proper functioning if they break down. Workers who set up one or a number of machines for other workers or who set up and personally operate a variety of machines are included here.

1. Precision Working: Using body members and/or tools or work aids to work, move, guide, or place objects or materials in situations where ultimate responsibility for the attainment of standards occurs and selection of appropriate tools, objects, or materials, and the adjustment of the tool to the task require exercise of considerable judgment.

2. Operating-Controlling: Starting, stopping, controlling, and adjusting the progress of machines or equipment. Operating machines involves setting up and adjusting the machine or material(s) as the work progresses. Controlling involves observing gauges, dials, etc., and turning valves and other devices to regulate factors such as temperature, pressure, flow of liquids, speed of pumps, and reactions of materials.

3. Driving-Operating: Starting, stopping, and controlling the actions of machines or equipment for which a course must be steered, or which must be guided, in order to fabricate, process, and/or move things or people. Involves such activities as observing gages and dials; estimating distances and determining speed and direction of other objects; turning cranks and wheels; pushing or pulling gear lifts or levers. Includes such machines as cranes, conveyor systems, tractors, furnace charging machines, paving machines and hoisting machines. Excludes manually powered machines, such as handtrucks and dollies, and power assisted machines, such as electric wheelbarrows and handtrucks.

4. Manipulating: Using body members, tools, or special devices to work, move, guide, or place objects or materials. Involves some latitude for judgment with regard to precision attained and selecting appropriate tool, object, or material, although this   readily manifest.

5. Tending: Starting, stopping, and observing the functioning of machines and equipment. Involves adjusting materials or controls of the machine, such as changing guides, adjusting timers and temperature gages, turning valves to allow flow of materials, and flipping switches in response to lights. Little judgment is involved in making these adjustments.

6. Feeding-Offbearing: Inserting, throwing, dumping, or placing materials in or removing them from machines or equipment which are automatic or tended or operated by other workers.

7. Handling: Using body members, handtools, and/or special devices to work, move or carry objects or materials.

283

Index

V
Vocabulary, 226

W
What Do You Want To Be Now That You're All Grown Up, vii
Writing skills, 271, 229-234

Fell's

Official Know-It-All Guide™

Check out these exciting titles in our Know-It-All™ series, available at your favorite bookstore:

- ☐ Fell's Official Know-It-All™ Guide: Advanced Hypnotism
- ☐ Fell's Official Know-It-All™ Guide: Advanced Magic
- ☐ Fell's Official Know-It-All™ Guide: The Art of Traveling Extravagantly & Nearly Free
- ☐ Fell's Official Know-It-All™ Guide: Budget Weddings
- ☐ Fell's Official Know-It-All™ Guide: Contract Bridge
- ☐ Fell's Official Know-It-All™ Guide: Coins 2003
- ☐ Fell's Official Know-It-All™ Guide: Cruises
- ☐ Fell's Official Know-It-All™ Guide: Defensive Divorce
- ☐ Fell's Official Know-It-All™ Guide: Dreams
- ☐ Fell's Official Know-It-All™ Guide: Easy Entertaining
- ☐ Fell's Official Know-It-All™ Guide: ESP Power
- ☐ Fell's Official Know-It-All™ Guide: Getting Rich & Staying Rich
- ☐ Fell's Official Know-It-All™ Guide: Health & Wellness
- ☐ Fell's Official Know-It-All™ Guide: Hypnotism
- ☐ Fell's Official Know-It-All™ Guide: Knots
- ☐ Fell's Official Know-It-All™ Guide: Let's Get Results, Not Excuses
- ☐ Fell's Official Know-It-All™ Guide: Magic for Beginners
- ☐ Fell's Official Know-It-All™ Guide: Money Management for College Students
- ☐ Fell's Official Know-It-All™ Guide: Mortgage Maze
- ☐ Fell's Official Know-It-All™ Guide: No Bull Selling
- ☐ Fell's Official Know-It-All™ Guide: Nutrition For a New America
- ☐ Fell's Official Know-It-All™ Guide: Online Investing
- ☐ Fell's Official Know-It-All™ Guide: Palm Reading
- ☐ Fell's Official Know-It-All™ Guide: Relationship Selling
- ☐ Fell's Official Know-It-All™ Guide: Secrets of Mind Power
- ☐ Fell's Official Know-It-All™ Guide: So, You Want to be a Teacher
- ☐ Fell's Official Know-It-All™ Guide: Super Power Memory
- ☐ Fell's Official Know-It-All™ Guide: Ultimate Beauty Recipes
- ☐ Fell's Official Know-It-All™ Guide: Wedding Planner
- ☐ Fell's Official Know-It-All™ Guide: Wisdom in the Office